Understanding Your Worst Enemy

by
Pastor Mel Bond

"And he said unto them, I beheld Satan as lightning fall from heaven," (Luke 10:18).

Dedication

This book is dedicated to my wife who has stood by me and supported me regardless of how hard and long our trials have been. Volumes of information could be given on the above statement, but I think it will be much better told when you hear the name Donna Jean Bond given much attention in heaven because of her life style and faithfulness while here on earth.

Biographical Sketch

My name is Mel Bond. I was born again June 17, 1958, at the age of eight. I fell away from the Lord a short time after my conversion and did not yield to Him again until I was 17 years old.

I married Donna Jean Hale on June 20, 1970. Donna and I began evangelizing in 1971 and pastored our first church in 1972.

Unfortunately, after going to Bible college, our ministry and lives still had very little foundation. In 1973, I received some of Rev. Kenneth Hagin's tapes and books, and from that time on, we have had purpose and direction. It is because of the foundation that we now have in God's Word and His Person that we have withstood hell's greatest attacks and still have a smile on our faces, peace in our hearts and love to give to whoever desires to receive it.

Foreword

Understanding Our Worst Enemy

Understanding that satan had an origin in heaven causes a person to know that satan is, "in one sense," extremely intelligent and organized for destruction.

When we see from the Scriptures the organized world order, system and kingdom that was his throne and jurisdiction on this earth when it was in its void stage, then we can understand the seriousness and obvious operation of satan as well as the underlying evil of his person.

From the time God said, "Let there be light," satan's domain was transferred to that of the first heaven. By understanding his past, we can understand how his kingdom operates and its motives today. In studying the Word of God, I found in Revelation 5:11, a figure given of one hundred trillion angels. This figure came after record was made of one-third of the angels being cast from heaven. Figuring mathematically, if the world had five billion people, and we divide the third of the angels up evenly with humanity, we can see a total of over 6.7 thousand fallen angels (which are now demons) assigned to each human being. Keep in mind that the primary function of demons is to kill, steal and destroy humanity.

Also keep in mind other accounts in the Scriptures in which angels are described as an innumerable company. Hebrews 12:22, describes such a company. This figure was also given after the third had been cast out of heaven. Ephesians talks about three other classifications or orders of demons, other than the one-third who are fallen angels or demons. I provide this information so the reader can better understand the seriousness of demonic warfare and begin to view it as a matter of life and death.

As we study the Scriptures as well as observe some manifestations in our world today, we can clearly see and understand the obvious manifestations of satan and his kingdom today. Just as sure as one can come to the conclusion that there are some obvious manifestations of satan, one can also learn from the Scriptures and the Holy Spirit some not-so-obvious manifestations or hidden operations of satan.

As never before Christians must understand that we are literally "at war" with satan and his kingdom. Christians MUST understand principles of warfare and weaponry to protect themselves, those they love and circumstances and substances that God has given them as believers.

As never before the believer must understand his armor and keep it on, because satan is intelligent and organized in knowing who has armor and weaponry assigned against him. When that person removes it to sleep or slumber, they will be defeated, even though once a victorious warrior.

The believer must be trained not to wait for the enemy to find them. But to be aggressive to discern the enemy as a bloodhound finds and stops a criminal. The Christian who only protects his immediate territory will experience very little victory in his life.

There is a discerning wisdom that can be gleaned from the Holy Scriptures and by walking with the Holy Spirit that will allow the common Christian to discern clearly the common, simple manifestations of satan and his kingdom.

There is a higher order of discernment which is like the simple order of discernment discussed earlier. But the higher order is more pronounced and more supernatural.

As never before, people need to know that satan is not playing games. He is playing for eternal keeps. The Christian who gives in to even the smallest sin is giving into satan. Worse yet, they are taking their first step towards being possessed. One must learn that discovering the riches of God's goodness to them is the secret of not even wanting the pleasures of sin that only last for a short time and then have a wage of torment.

The weakest member of the body of Christ has advantage over the most powerful evil spirit. The believer must learn the simplicity of his authority and how to use that authority to discern and cast out the microscopic beginnings of evil-spirit schemes.

When a Christian learns the simplicity of what God's armor is and how to wear and use it, they simply will develop the fullness of God in this world and will fulfill God's mind and purpose. This will cause the Body of Christ to walk in God's glory (literally, His reputation) which is divine joy, victory and life.

Contents

Introduction

Too often Christians are defeated in many areas of their lives because they fail to understand the realm of satan and his kingdom. To be victorious, they must learn to discern and cast evil spirits from situations.

The purpose of this book is to help the Body of Christ clearly and accurately understand the presence and operation of Satan and demon spirits. We need to become keenly aware that this is the time in which Revelation 12:17 is being fulfilled. In this passage of Scripture, we see that satan is extremely angry and is making war with those who keep the commandments of God and have the testimony of Jesus.

For the information above to be well established, a higher truth is to be understood – that is the necessity of equipping the saints with revelation knowledge concerning the gift of discerning spirits, along with other revelation truths that expose the enemy. Saints also need the knowledge from God's Word that a child of God is more than a conqueror through Christ Jesus.

The shortest summation of this book would be this:

If someone you loved dearly were being tortured by

someone who was unclean and evil, and you were present and able to stop this evil, no doubt you would. First, a violence would rise in your spirit and then you would do in the natural what you were picturing and experiencing in your spirit. By the same token, if we would treat every spiritual situation that is contrary to us as Bible believers, in the same way as we perceive them in our spirits, we would be victorious in all walks of life.

CHAPTER *1*

Origin Of Satan In Heaven

We need to know our enemy. Isaiah 14:16-17, states that the day will come in which Satan will shake everything that can be shaken; and only those who are established in God's Word will be able to stand. In talking about these same days, Jesus warned that if God did not shorten the time, the very elect would be lost.

I do not believe that teachings on demonology should be the predominant teaching of Scriptures, but we need to understand there is a season for everything. For every word in the Bible there is also a season. Now is the time for the Body of Christ to rise up with supernatural, overcoming strength for victory in every situation. Understanding every possible thing we can about the enemy of our person will be a giant step in accomplishing this goal.

Know Your Enemy –

The failures of the Vietnam War and the great losses we suffered there, are prime examples of what can happen when we fail to know and understand our enemies. We knew very little about our enemies in Vietnam, so we had many casualties as a result. Now, we are in a spiritual war – the worst war Christianity has ever been in or will be in. We are in the war of Revelation 12:17, in which Satan directs GREAT WRATH toward those that know the Word, use the Word and speak the Word with God's anointing and results. It is the greatest era of all time and the most victorious for the Body of Christ. However, victory will be repressed or delayed unless we go on to maturity in the Lord. Learning as much as we can about satan is a necessary part of the maturing process. Satan means business. He isn't playing games. We need to understand his character and operations just the way an elite combat troop would understand its enemy in the heat of battle.

In January 1973, the Lord appeared to me in a vision and told me that for the rest of my life, I would be confronted with demonic spirits in an unprecedented manner, but that He (Jesus) would always be by my side, enabling me to be victorious.

This book reveals many of the truths the Lord has taught me over the years by visions, experiences, study of His Word and, of course, by measuring everything by His Holy Word. When Christians begin to come to the knowledge of just how active satan is today and how with cunning and subtle tactics he plots a hideous end for all who follow him, they will become immeasurably more successful at being partakers of the nature of God.

"Grace and peace be multiplied unto you through the knowledge of God, and of Jesus our Lord,

*"According as his divine power **"HATH GIVEN"** unto us all things that pertain unto life and godliness, through the knowledge of him that hath called us to glory and virtue:*

"Whereby are given unto us exceeding great and precious promises: that by these ye might be partakers of the divine nature, having escaped the corruption that is in the world through lust," (2 Peter 1:2-4).

A high priority in writing this book is to give the

2

child of God a sound understanding of the fact that, as they submit to God and His Word, they can resist Satan's worst attack against them and HE WILL HAVE TO FLEE IN TERROR. Satan is horrified of the child of God who knows the Word of God and how to use it. No weapon formed against such a one will prosper, and he will be able, with the Word, to condemn every tongue that might arise against him.

"No weapon that is formed against thee shall prosper; and every tongue that shall rise against thee in judgment thou shalt condemn. This is the heritage of the servants of the Lord, and their righteousness is of me, saith the Lord," (Isaiah 54:17).

We have authority over the devil, but we need to understand him and learn even the smallest operation of his person. As we look at how he operates, at his origination and character, we then understand how he is working. If satan ever destroys us in any fashion, it will be primarily through something small. (It is the little foxes that spoil the vine.) For example, every church that has ever been destroyed, was not destroyed from the outside but from within. If the laws of the land would come and try to shut our churches down, in a week's time, we would double in size; in three week's time, we would triple. It would be news and people would want to know what in the world was happening. They would come out of great curiosity; and then the Lord would show up as usual and they wouldn't be able to resist the riches of His goodness toward them.

What will divide us is something small from within, such as a demon of criticism, gossip, unteachableness or noncommitment. By the way, these are the leading spirits assigned to all churches that teach and preach the Word. These are extremely powerful demon spirits that first destroy lives, then families, then ministries and last, churches. And satan has been very successful in doing

3

this for years because it all starts with little words that are satan inspired. It is the born-again, Bible-reading, Bible-quoting, tongue-talking people who have unintentionally allowed these spirits to use them. They were easily trapped because, **AT FIRST, THESE WORDS "APPEAR" SO SMALL AND HARMLESS,** certainly not satanically-inspired. But the Bible is plain about idle (useless) words, foolish (clowny, silly) words, vain (empty, unprofitable) words, corrupt (worthless, bad, hurtful) communications.

In Matthew 12 and Ephesians 4 and 5, we can plainly see that one who yields to such speaking is being used by an evil spirit as much as an adulterer or whoremonger. Dear friends, if the words of our mouths are not ministering unmerited favor (blessings undeserved) and building others up and drawing them closer to the Lord, they are corrupt words or satan-inspired words leading to a damnable end for the speaker. A.A. Allen once said that the GREATEST KEY TO REVIVAL is the words from our mouths.

"But I say unto you, That every idle word that men shall speak, they shall give account thereof in the day of judgment," (Matthew 12:36).

"Let no corrupt communication proceed out of your mouth, but that which is good to the use of edifying, that it may minister grace unto the hearers," (Ephesians 4:29).

Know Where Your Enemy Lives –

We must understand how subtle satan is, how he operates in the microscopic, not-so-obvious areas and even from a Scriptural standpoint. As we look at Ezekiel 28, keep in mind that these verses cannot be referring to a natural man. Let us examine the Scriptures and I will show you why. The best interpretation of the Bible is itself. We need to compare Scripture with Scripture. In looking at the first three verses, one would think it is talking about a human being. However, as we look at the remainder of the chapter, we find it is talking about satan himself.

"The word of the Lord came again unto me saying,

"Son of man, say unto the prince of Tyrus, Thus saith the Lord God; Because thine heart is lifted up, and thou hast said, I am a god, I sit in the seat of God, in the midst of the seas; yet thou art a man, and not "God" though thou set thine heart as the heart of God:

"Behold thou art wiser than Daniel; there is no secret that they can hide from thee," (Ezekiel 28:1-3).

Who is this individual in Verse 2, who is called the prince of Tyrus? Bible scholars have long recognized that satan and demonic spirits work within certain geographical locations. I believe in this passage the prince of Tyrus is satan himself who was assigned to Tyrus. And you will see why I believe this as we examine the chapter. Satan was the prince of Tyrus in the realm of the spirit.

The Apostle Paul talks about a third heaven as does the book of Revelation and other passages. Obviously if there is a third heaven, there must be a second and a first. The first heaven is the atmospheric heaven right above our heads which contains the air we breathe, etc. Satan and his kingdom abide in the first heaven.

The Bible tells us in 2 Corinthians 10:3-5 that, *"...we walk in the flesh, we do not war after the flesh:*

"(For the weapons of our warfare are not carnal, but mighty through God to the pulling down of strongholds;)

"Casting down imaginationos, and every high thing that exalteth itself against the knowledge of God...."

So many times in the past, because of tradition, we have thought of satan as being in the belly of the earth beneath us. However, his kingdom is actually in the first heaven that abides over our heads, with different geographical locations being inhabited by different demonic spirits. In this particular time and location, satan was the prince of Tyrus. You can also see this noted in Daniel 10, in greater detail.

When going from community to community, especially when changing geographical locations with a good deal of distance or as you drive from one state to another, have you noticed that the same problems in one state do not exist in another? As my wife and I traveled in the early '70's from state to state holding Gospel services, we noticed this phenomena. One area would be strong with, for example, tobacco, in which you would see even small children using it in different forms. Then we would go into another geographic area and see, not tobacco addiction but pornography. By observation it was plain that different spirits were stronger in different locations.

How do we know that Ezekiel 28 is not talking about a man rather than a demon spirit or satan himself? Scriptures will reveal the answer. Verse 3 of Ezekiel 28 states, "Behold, thou art wiser than Daniel; there is no secret that they can hide from thee."

A human being would not possess this type of knowledge. No one person is capable of knowing all secrets. Therefore, the prince of Tyrus had to be some type of supernatural being, possessing the ability to know all secrets. Nothing could be hid from him; the Bible clearly says so. Notice that this passage is from the Old Testament, and we that are born again today are of the New Testament. The good news is, satan does not know everything about the New Testament believer. In essence, we have secrets about which he knows nothing.

1 Corinthians 14:2 says that when we speak in tongues, we speak divine secrets. Ephesians 3:19 says there is love of God that passeth knowledge. So if we speak in tongues, we speak knowledge satan knows nothing about, And if we will walk in God's love, satan will never find us.

Now look at Ezekiel 28:8:

"They shall bring thee down to the pit, and thou shalt die the deaths of them that are slain in the midst of seas."

The death described here is a spiritual death. Again, Scripture proves that this prince could not be human. In addition, this being continues to live in the present time. No one has ever lived that long except God. Even more compelling is the fact that this prince continues to live on even after he dies. The Bible talks about a spiritual death that is in essence an eternal separation from God. Such a death certainly applies to satan who is eternally separated from God's goodness, mercy and indwelling nature.

"Wilt thou yet say before him that slayeth thee, I am God? But thou shalt be a man, and not God, in the hand of him that slayeth thee....

"Thou hast been in Eden the garden of God;...." (Ezekiel 28:9 and 13).

So this individual had, at some time in the past, been in the garden of God. Since no man has been in the garden of God, we must be reading about a supernatural individual. Let's continue reading in Verse 13:

"...Every precious stone was thy covering, the sardis, topaz and the diamond, the beryl, the onyx, and the jasper, the sapphire, the emerald, and the carbuncle, and gold: the workmanship of thy tabrets and of thy pipes was prepared in thee in the day that thou was created."

Man is not created – he is born. Of course, Adam and Eve were created by God but everyone since has been born and not created. The Bible states that this prince was created so he could not have been a natural human being. He had to be a spiritual being. Note again the latter part of Verse 13: "...tabrets and ...pipes were prepared in thee in the day that thou was created."

So he was created with some musical intruments in him. As you study you will find that tabrets are a tambourine-type instrument. The pipes refer to some other type of musical instrument. No doubt satan used these when he was in the garden of God. Some people believe the devil was one of the main worship leaders in heaven.

We know these musical instruments were created within him. That tells us something else about the nature of satan. You may have noticed that much of today's secular music is ordained by satan. The devil still uses music. Consider the nature of some music. What body language does it draw attention to? What are the words of the music? What type of atmosphere does it create? What type of life style do the promoters and supporters lead? Obviously, satan uses and ordains much of today's music.

By the same token, some of today's music is God-ordained and Scriptural in nature, clearly glorifying our great God and Savior. We can also understand by the Scriptures that God invented music, which lets us know satan was used for music in the garden of God.

Verse 14 says, *"Thou art the anointed cherub...."*

Here he is called an anointed cherub. The word "cherub" refers to one particular order of angelic beings; so he was a particular type or order of angel. Again, he could not, according to these descriptions, be a natural individual.

Why Satan Fell –

Continuing with Verse 14 and into 15, *"...that covereth; and I have set thee so: thou wast upon the holy mountain of God; thou hast walked up and down in the midst of the stones of fire.*

"Thou wast perfect in thy ways...."

NO HUMAN BEING HAS EVER BEEN PERFECT in the sense that God said this individual was – "...perfect in thy ways from the day that thou wast created...."

Again, this prince was in the mountain of God and is

8

about to be cast out because of his profanity.

"...and I will destroy thee, O covering cherub, from the midst of the stones of fire.

"Thine heart was lifted up because of thy beauty...." (Ezekiel 28:16,17).

The devil fell because of pride; and pride is still a tool he uses today to cause people to fall.

"Pride goeth before destructon, and an haughty spirit before a fall," (Proverbs 16:18).

Remember the words in Ezekiel 28:2: *"...because thine heart is lifted up...."* So the devil was lifted up with pride because of his beauty. Everybody is beautiful in one fashion or another, whether it is physical, mental, socially or whatever. Too often pride sneaks in and says, "You're better than they. You know more than them. You have more than they, etc."

Brother Kenneth Hagin tells the story of a demon-possessed lady who had been a preacher's wife. (The fact that we are Christians does not in any way exempt us from being tempted and attacked by the devil. We cannot be possessed by the devil and be a Christian; but we can certainly be harassed or oppressed by him.) Anyway, this woman was very attractive; and every time she was in front of a mirror, she would look at herself and a thought would enter her mind: "You sure are an attractive lady. If you weren't married; if you weren't in the ministry, you could have all sorts of attention from men as well as really achieve in life. You could have a much more attractive husband and be much more stable financially."

These thoughts persisted and she enjoyed entertaining them. She enjoyed the ego boost they gave her. The devil is very stupid for choosing to leave heaven for eternity, but in many ways he displays a serpent's wisdom. He begins telling people how intelligent they are; how great they are; how much better they are than everyone else.

So the lady continued to think and have pleasure with

these thoughts. What she was doing was allowing evil spirits to have an entrance into her life. After a certain time span, she began to have an affair with another man. As time went on she began to love her beauty more than she loved her husband and then more than she loved God. The devil isn't going to come in some obvious way to trap us, such as saying, "Worship me by killing someone you love and sacrificing them to me," No. First he will come in with just a subtle thought that will lift your ego. He longs to take a truth and pervert it. Neither is the devil allowed to use any new trick; he uses the same age-old tricks over and over. The same faults that caused him to fall are the same ones with which he deceives humanity today.

So because of his beauty, the devil fell.

"Thine heart was lifted up because of thy beauty, thou hast corrupted thy wisdom by reason of thy brightness: I will cast thee to the ground, I will lay thee before kings, that they may behold thee.

"Thou hast defiled thy sanctuaries by the multitude of thine iniquities, by the iniquity of thy traffick; therefore will I bring forth a fire from the midst of thee, it shall devour thee, and I will bring thee to ashes upon the earth in the sight of all them that behold thee," (Ezekiel 28:17, 18).

Notice the words, "I will cast thee to the ground," in Verse 17. This individual was cast out of heaven to the ground. This supports what Jesus said in Luke 10:18: *"...I beheld Satan as lightning fall from heaven."* We also see correlation in Revelation 12. When satan was cast out of heaven, one-third of the angels were cast out with him.

"And there appeared another wonder in heaven; and behold a great red dragon, having seven heads and ten horns, and seven crowns upon his heads," (Revelation 12:3).

The great red dragon refers to satan.

"And his tail drew the third part of the stars of heav-

en...." Again we see reference to the third of the angels who fell with satan.

"...and did cast them to the earth: and the dragon stood before the woman...." (Revelation 12:4).

Did you notice how the same train of thought is used in Ezekiel 28? It is also used in Isaiah 14, as well as Luke 10:18. The "stars of heaven" noted in Ezekiel 28:4 were cast to the earth from their abode with God. So the dragon and a third of the stars(angels) who were in abode with God were cast to the earth. Revelation 4 continues to describe a war in heaven. Michael, his angels and the archangels fought against the dragon, and the dragon fought against God's angels. One third of the stars or angels were defeated. Satan fell along with all angels who joined forces with him in fighting Michael and the angels of heaven. These angels of profanity, along with the dragon, did not prevail against Michael and the other two-thirds of the angels who abode with God; and they were cast down.

"And prevailed not; neither was their place found any more in heaven.

"And the great dragon was cast out, that old serpent, called the devil, and satan..." (Revelation 12: 8,9).

I am not grasping at straws. The Scriptures spell it out plainly. That's why it is so important to read the whole Bible. Sometimes you read something in the Bible and you say, "Well, you know, this is using a figure of speech here. The dragon could symbolize anything."

However, as you read the remainder of the Bible, you find it spelled out clearly that the dragon is the devil himself. Anyone who knows and truly understands the Bible, can prove that which is good by using Scripture or disprove that which is not of God by using Scripture. All we need to know about truth is in God's Word. But no one can disprove sound doctrine if they disprove or prove it in the manner Jesus did; and that is simply this: Does the teaching glorify God? Are there at least three Scriptures

11

that support the doctrine and does it correlate with the main thrust of the Bible (John 3:16)? Does the thought agree with the main idea of the whole chapter in which it is found? If you will use this philosophy, you can disprove unsound doctrine and prove sound doctrine.

After looking closely at Ezekiel 28 and the other Scriptures herein provided, it should be obvious that the "prince" described here is not a mere man, but rather is satan himself.

CHAPTER 2

Satan's Kingdom in Operation Today

Where is satan's kingdom today? How does he operate?

"In whom the god of this world hath blinded the minds of them which believe not, lest the light of the glorious gospel of Christ, who is the image of God, should shine unto them," (2 Corinthians 4:4).

The god of this world, satan, has blinded the minds of those who believe not. The devil will blind the eyes of people to keep them from seeing the truth. He is a "god," but he is not our God. He is not Jehovah God; he is not Almighty God; he is not the God of kindness, gentleness and goodness. But he is a "little god." You will notice the small "g" I use when referring to satan as a god. Even the King James Bible does not capitalize it because there is only one capitalized God – and there is only one true God.

Satan is a little god of evil. A God of goodness is not going to blind your eyes from understanding the light of the Gospel. The true God is a God of lovingkindness beyond our understanding, and His divine will is that none perish. (See 2 Peter 3:9.) It is His will that all humanity be saved and come to the full knowledge of the truth. (See 2 Timothy 2:4.) The true God will open the eyes of our understanding so we can see the light of the glorious Gospel and possess this treasure in earthen vessels. (See 2 Corinthians 4:6-7.)

Your Weapon Is The Word of God –

My little girls learned at three years of age how to take authority over the devil when he tried to create sickness and disease in their bodies. I have documents in my office proving the healing of one of my children.

One of my daughters, at age nine, was declared legally blind, and this was documented by medical science. Her vision was 20/200. Her eyesight persistently grew worse. (Persistency is another characteristic of satan.) We need to be more persistant than he is. So I taught her the Word of God and how we have authority over demon spirits that would try to create blindness. Now I have a document by the same medical physician stating that she has 20/20 vision.

Donna and I have three children on the earth with us now, our oldest being 20 years old this year of 1992. We have taught them all since they began to talk to memorize the Word of God, and they all are a great threat to satan and his kingdom.

"Hell from beneath is moved for thee to meet thee at thy coming: it stirreth up the dead for thee, even all the chief ones of the earth; it hath raised up from their thrones all the kings of the nations," (Isaiah 14:9).

How would you like to have the whole pit of hell moved and waiting for you? Satan knows this and I believe this is one of the reasons in these last days he has such great wrath. Because misery likes company.

"All they shall speak and say unto thee, Art thou also become weak as we? art thou become like unto us?" (Isaiah

14

14:10).

In other words, he was pretty powerful. He has become weak as the weakest people in the pit of hell. In fact, he is going to become weaker as we read on in this chapter.

"Thy pomp is brought down to the grave, and the noise of thy viols: the worm is spread under thee, and the worms cover thee.

"How art thou fallen from heaven, O Lucifer, son of the morning! how art thou cut down to the ground, which didst weaken the nations!

"For thou hast said in thine heart, I will ascend into heaven, I will exalt my throne above the stars of God: I will sit also upon the mount of the congregation, in the sides of the north:

"I will ascend above the heights of the clouds; I will be like the most High," (Isaiah 14:11-14).

Satan Had a Kingdom That Was Destroyed –

Notice again he had a throne. A throne represents dominion. It represents a kingdom, a system; and he had a world system. He said, "I will exalt my throne above the throne of God. I will ascend above the heights of the clouds; I will be like the Most High." Here is the age-old voice of the devil. He will be like God. Again we see that same old train of thought taking place – pride and dominion; "I" am going to do something for ME. "I," not for God, but "I" am going to do it for me. This spirit tries to creep into good ministries. "I" am going to build this ministry. "I" am going to build this church. When "I" gets in the picture and humility goes out, you can know it is doomed for failure.

Read Verses 15, 16, 17 of Isaiah 14. Is this the little wormy wimp that has been brought low? The weakest of the weak sees he is a wimp. He has no authority over us when we know the Word of God. Jesus said, if you con-

15

tinue in the Word, then you are my disciples; and then you shall know the truth and the truth shall set you free (John 8:31,32).

Where Satan Now Rules –

Just as sure as satan was in heaven and had an evil, organized kingdom on this earth, we must know that he has a kingdom in the first heaven that "IS NOW" very much in operation and thoroughly organized for humanity's destruction. He is the author of darkness, evil and destruction in this earth today. And until we put a stop to his operation, sickness, disease, premature death, financial poverty, marriages and lives will continually be destroyed. (See John 10:10; Psalm 17:4; 1 Corinthians 10:10; Job 2:7; Acts 10:38; Luke 13:16; and Matthew 12:22 – just a few Scriptures to support the fact that satan is in operation today.)

I wish people could see into the realm of the spirit at least a couple of times in their lives. It would cause them to be more serious about life, about God and His Word, about eternity and about the reality of the spirit world which is more real than physical.

For several years I had chest pains, many times so severe that thoughts would race into my mind that, "You only have seconds to live!" The pain was greater than any pain I had ever experienced. The first time it happened, my wife was in the hospital with our newborn, now oldest daughter, Cherish. I was at the breakfast table at home and the pain was so severe, I believed I would die in just a few seconds. A thought came to my mind, "If you move even your smallest finger on your right hand, it will overtax your body to the degree that pain will increase more than you can imagine, and then you will die."

I said, within myself, "I might as well die praising God!" So I lifted both arms to praise the Lord. As soon

16

as I did, immediately, 100 percent of the pain and every symptom left. My theology was not accurate as it is today, but thank God the basis of it was. God will meet you where you are, providing your heart is right.

The pain came back again about six months later, not as severe, But as the years went by, I had pain even more severe at times. In 1973 I learned from some of Brother Kenneth Hagin's books and tapes how to believe and understand the Word of God more accurately. I began to notice a great deal of victory. However, as I grew in the Word, I noticed the pain coming back and getting worse to the point I would black out. I continued to believe God's Word, thinking, *"I'd rather believe God's Word and die than live and not believe it."*

There is a much worse death than physical death. In fact, physical death is something to look forward to. For the child of God, it is a great time of victory. However, those who are very much alive physically but do not believe God's Word, have only a shell of a life. They are really quite dead. So understand, the more of God's Word you know, the more you can believe and the more abundant life you will have.

Several years later during the night, I awakened because of the severe chest pain and plainly saw a demon spirit standing over me laughing demoniacally. He had fingers that were at least nine inches long and his index finger on his right hand was deep into my chest and into my heart. At that moment, faster than the human mind can think, knowledge from God came to me just as He always does in these visions. And the Lord said, "This is your problem, this evil spirit of infirmity."

I then rebuked the spirit, and he slowly pulled his finger out of my heart and chest. As he did, he began to vanish and the pain started decreasing instantly as he removed his finger out of my heart and chest. But it was at least a half hour before all the symptoms left. We must understand who our enemy is, where he is and how he operates or we will never be victorious. There are spirits for every kind of problem that exists, and until we learn to expose them and violently deal with them, we will not experience God's best for our lives. We are at war with satan and his kingdom, and most Christians do not even know it!

Satan's Present Kingdom in the Heavenlies

Revelation 12:12 is a passage of Scripture which I am strongly convinced is for this day and time. The Word of God says, *"...Woe to the inhabitants of the earth and of the sea! for the devil is come down unto you, having great wrath, because he knoweth that he hath but a short time."*

A primary understanding to be promoted in this book is that we have authority over all the enemy as Jesus proclaimed in Luke 10:19:

"Behold, I give unto you power to tread on serpents and scorpions, and over all the power of the enemy: and nothing shall by any means hurt you."

In this passage, serpents and scorpions refer to demonic powers; satanic powers. This Scripture remains relevant today. God has given us authority over all the power of the enemy. Many people think they know the power of God; but those who know the power of God know how to use it and also know that satan is no match for the least member of the Body of Christ. He is horrified and flees and trembles when they exercise their God-given rights.

There has been much good teaching in the Body of Christ in the last 20 years, but some spirit-filled Christians are using Scripture and the Name of Jesus too much like they would use a rabbit's foot. And that is why they are having rabbit-foot results – nothing is coming to pass. Hands are laid on people and they say, "In the Name of Jesus," but there are no results. We see two problems here: Number One, people are being used by demon forces as much as they are desiring to be used of the Holy Spirit; and some are not even conscience of it (but will be after this statement).

"Out of the same mouth proceedeth blessing and cursing. My brethren, these things ought not so to be," (James 3:10).

OUT OF THE SAME MOUTH proceedeth blessing and cursing. Verse 15 of James 2 calls such things "devilish."

Number Two: If I posess something, I should be able to know if I have given it away or not. I know that we can lay hands on people in faith, but there comes a time when we ought to grow up and learn of things in the spirit. The realm of the spirit should be more real to us than the physical realm. In the natural realm I started knowing I had given something when I was just a child. The Name of Jesus and words that are in agreement with that Name are to be used more than just on Sunday morning and in times of emergency. It is a way of life. We need to get serious with God to have serious results.

I have been reluctant to teach on many of these truths over the years, I guess, for a couple of reasons. For example, I noticed every time I would teach on the subject, I began having all kinds of problems. So I figured the Body of Christ was not ready for such teaching. But most recently, I have lost some people who have been and still are very dear to me. Satan's work has been clearly seen, and I am extremely angry at him. I am going to expose his work and everything I know about him in order to destroy it.

The devil is a very intelligent being. He is well organized and quite powerful. But again, I'm saying he is no match for the smallest child that knows how to submit to God and resist the devil. By the same token, the age-old Christian who has lived and knows the Word of God but doesn't submit to it, is no match for the devil. I mean absolutely no match.

Look in Isaiah 14:16 where reference is being made to satan:

"They that see thee shall narrowly look upon thee, and consider thee, saying, Is this the man that made the earth to tremble, that did shake kingdoms...."

See, a person is no match for the devil outside of the supernatural power of God. That is why it is reasonable to ask, "How in the world could anyone possibly do this?" Scripture says, "He made the earth to tremble." I'm not trying to exalt the devil; I'm exposing him so people can see that they must become very serious in resisting him. We cannot live a 99 percent carnal life and rebuke the devil and expect him to leave. He isn't going to leave. He makes the earth to tremble and shakes kingdoms; makes the world as a wilderness and destroys the cities thereof; opens not the house of the prisoners. We must get serious with the devil. And the way to do this is to get serious with God and His Word. Then satan will be no match for you!

A Vision of Jesus –

The first vision I had of the Lord Jesus Christ was in October of 1973. Jesus took me into the realm of the spirit and down a corridor. There I saw all sorts of demons as far as the eye could see in every direction. Demons of every hideous nature imaginable. As I was walking down this corridor with Jesus on my right side, one very hideous, evil-looking demon with long fingers and finger nails (perhaps the same demon who had his finger in my

21

chest several years later) came up to me as though he hated me and wanted to violently destroy me. Just being in that place was horrifying enough; but when this demon came rushing into my face acting as though he was going to claw my eyes out, I became fearful. At that moment Jesus sensed my fright and gently squeezed my right hand which He was holding. As He did, I looked up at Him and He said, "The rest of your life, you will have dealings of this nature," meaning encounters with evil spirits. "But," he continued, "I will always be with you."

When Jesus spoke these words, there was no more torment of fear, and the evil spirit vanished. Since that time, on a very frequent basis, I have experienced the realm of the spirit. On rare occasions, I have seen angels. Predominantly, just as Jesus said, I see, hear, feel and perceive demons. By observation I have noticed the greater depth of living in the spirit. The gift of discerning spirits has been more frequently in operation and manifestation. I have also noticed that the greater degree to which I live in the spirit, the more accurate I am in my perception of demons (understanding their purpose) and the less torment they manifest toward me. This is Biblical, and since satan and sin are synonymous terms, sin brings torment. But walking more in the spirit means yielding less to satan-sin-torment.

There was a time when I had to be very forceful, even audible and physical in order to exercise authority over them. However, I began to realize that it does no good to try to hit them or do anything of a physical nature, as I tried many times to do. They would only laugh. There is a great lesson to learn from this, and that is – deal with spiritual problems on a spiritual level and with spiritual weapons. Now I only have to think or release an authority out of my spirit, and they are horrified and leave.

Around 1986, a demon spirit stood in front of me in the kitchen of the home we now live in. This demon was a messenger of Eldaah. He was extremely angry looking, very strong and sweaty. He said, "Eldaah is extremely mad because you are still breathing." Then he vanished. I really never gave the visitation much thought except to reinforce my thinking that humanity's biggest problem is spiritual.

But just the other day I thought about this experience and looked up the name Eldaah in one of my concordances in order to find the name in the Bible. Many spirits have scriptural names because many of them are fallen angels. The name "Eldaah" is mentioned two times in the Bible in reference to a son of a Midianite. It speaks of his nature as being the same as this particular demon that appeared to me. Demons are real; satan is real; but the Body of Christ has predominantly acted like the devil and demons are not real. That is probably one of the devil's greatest tools – trying to get Christians to believe that demons are dormant or nonexistent. Demons' greatest goals are to make you what they are. People are badly mistaken if they think that anger is just something in their genes. Anger is a spirit. And if it can use you, its next step is to let another spirit into your life who is worse, such as hate.

Guard Your Thought Life –

Evil spirits do not always come in obvious ways, as we will study in greater detail later on. They first come in with thoughts. That's the reason the Bible says, "The weapons of our warfare are not carnal, but they are mighty through God to the pulling down of strongholds, casting down imaginations and every high thing that exalts itself above the knowledge of God, and bringing every thought into the obedience of Christ, which is the Word of God." (See 2 Corinthians 10:4,5).

Demonic activity first begins in the thoughts. A demon will come in with a thought which can build in your life until that demon has destroyed you, if you allow it. That is their ultimate goal – to destroy humanity.

Earlier, we looked at how satan had a kingdom on this earth that was destroyed when God said, "Let there be light." So where is his kingdom now? In Matthew 12:26, people were accusing Jesus of being used by demonic powers Himself, and He said, "If I cast out satan in the name of satan, satan's kingdom will be divided against itself."

You will notice Jesus acknowledged here that satan has a kingdom. Also notice in the chapter before (Matthew 11:12) that Jesus said, "The kingdom of heaven suffereth violence and the violent take it by force."

As we study the context of this chapter and other Scriptures along this same train of thought, we see there is a heaven with which we are supposed to get violent. We have authority over certain situations in that heaven. That particular heaven withholds blessings from being manifested to us. It hinders us from having things that God has already given us. (See 2 Peter 1:2-4.) You can readily understand with your common sense, as well as coinciding that train of thought with the Word of God, that we do not have to get violent with God, the abode of God. It is unscriptural to get violent against the abode of God as well as useless. We do not have to get violent with God in order to take something we need. He has already given us all things that pertain to life and Godlikeness. We do not have to get mad with God.

So immediately your mind begins to think, "There must be another heaven?" You are correct. Colossians 1:13 says we have been delivered from the power of darkness and translated unto the kingdom of His dear Son. The word "power" here is not the same "power" used predominantly throughout the Scriptures. The word "power" in this Scripture is co-equal in the Greek with "magistrate," "jurisdiction," and "heavenly." So you could say it this way and be absolutely correct in accordance to the inspired Word of God: "We have been delivered from magistrates of darkness. We have been delivered from the heavenly darkness and translated into the kingdom of His dear Son." So we begin to see that satan has a kingdom, a magistrate and a jurisdiction. That tells me he is an intelligent creature, very well organized. He is also quite powerful, if he is king of a jurisdiction or kingdom. And he is. We are so foolish not to expose our enemy; not to understand that there is an enemy against us.

My human sensibilities tell me to just teach about God, heaven, his angels, the joy of God and things of that nature. Take, a young man, for example, and send him to the best military school on the face of the earth; but do not warn him about the enemy he will soon face. It will not matter how well-trained he is physically or militarily, he will be destroyed during the first hour of battle, if he does not know his enemy. That is what happened in Vietnam. We did not know our enemy nor jungle warfare that well. And many of our troops were horribly destroyed because of it.

We need to know about the enemy of our souls; the worst enemy of our being. Learn about him. How does he think? How does he operate? Where does he live? What does he live on? What are his habits? What are his strong points? What are his weak points? He is your worst enemy; his primary purpose is to destroy you. Don't play games with him; don't ever trust him, even a little. Learn everything you can about him and defeat him on every count, because you can. You absolutely can.

So, where is satan now? It is very plain, from the Scriptures I've given and others as well, that he has a kingdom. But where is his kingdom now? First of all we need to establish a little foundation before we can understand where his kingdom is. In 2 Corinthians 12:2, the Bible talks about the third heaven. The Apostle Paul is saying,

"I knew a man that was caught up into the third heaven." If there is a third heaven, there has to be a second and a first. As you study the Book of Revelation from the first chapter to the last, you will find that it talks about a heaven that is the abode of God, the same place John, on the Island of Patmos, was taken up into. This is where God lives and where His angels abide. This is where you are going when you die, if Jesus is the Lord of your life on this earth. (See Romans 10:9,10.)

The Second Heaven –

There is a multitude of Scriptures to support the existence of a second heaven where the stars, moon and sun are located. Genesis 22:17 talks about the stars of heaven. Many Scriptures show that there is a solar heaven. You will find there is a particular heaven totally different from this solar heaven. It is a heaven where the angels abide with God. So immediately you can see there is a third and a second heaven. So if there is a third and a second, there has to be a first. The first heaven is where satan and his kingdom is. Again, look at Ephesians 6:12: "...we wrestle not against flesh and blood, but against principalities, against powers, against the rulers of the darkness of this world, against spiritual wickedness in high places (or the heavenlies)." "High places" here is co-equal in meaning to the term "heavenlies."

Spiritual wickedness does not exist in the third heaven, the abode of God. So only one heaven remains, the atmospheric heaven immediately over our heads. As we quoted earlier, 2 Corinthians 10:3-5, says we must cast down the imaginations and every high thing, pulling down strongholds. We do this through prayer and interceding as the Holy Spirit reveals what the strongholds are over individuals, situations, cities.

In the Body of Christ, we have dealt with problems

many times by dealing with people or by intellectually trying to resolve problems, only to be disappointed when we had little results or things grew worse. The real problem is the devil and his kingdom of darkness, destruction, havoc, etc. We need to learn to walk in the spirit in such great depths that we can learn to discern and know how to deal with hindering, evil spirits directly, rather than trying to deal with a person or situation that seems to be the problem.

This is why we have gotten things in such a mess in the past; we have not dealt with the root of the problems we face. Many times people or situations are influenced by an evil spirit who is the source of their problem. In fact, because of my studies and experiences, I believe if there is a problem of any kind, we can know there is a spirit influencing somewhere.

As we go on, it is plain to understand that the first heaven is the atmospheric heaven and that's where satan and his kingdom reside. .

Worship God Alone –

"And he put down the idolatrous priests, whom the kings of Judah had ordained to burn incense in the high places in the cities of Judah, and in the places round about Jerusalem; them also that burned incense unto Baal, to the sun, and to the moon, and to the planets, and to all the host of heaven," (2 Kings 23:5).

How many people realize that it is wrong to burn incense in an idolatrous way? Such is the doctrines of devils. The priests were involved in doctrines of devils. It says, "...them also that burned incense unto Baal." In studying Baal, you will find he also was a demonic figure.

So we know this Scripture is not talking about the third heaven because that would be out of context. Everything else is demonic. To lift the thought, "the hosts of heaven," out and say that it refers to those in the abode of God would be taking Scripture out of context. No, they were rebuking them; they were stopping their evil doing. So it would be out of context for all these others to be evil and one to be of God. For one thing, we are not even supposed to worship the host of heaven. There is only one person we are supposed to worship and that is God Almighty. We must not even worship angels with all their splendor and might, regardless of how holy their job might be. The Scriptures are plain as to whom our worship must be directed.

"But though we, or an angel from heaven, preach any other gospel unto you than that which we have preached unto you, let him be accursed," (Galatians 1:8).

An order of angels exists, however, that seek to be worshipped, as the Apostle Paul warned. This is the one-third that was cast down with satan. They are the highest order of satan's angels and their primary ambition is to have God's position. Such an angel appeared to me one time, and he looked like the perfect order of religion. I want you to know this spirit was glowing. He looked perfect. Every hair on his head was in place. There were no wrinkles in his clothing. His speech was perfect; he was extremely dignified looking and sounding. He appeared as perfect as God Himself. He stood before me and told me, "The teachings that you are promoting concerning the grace of God are extreme and out of context with the Scriptures. I am here to correct you."

I had such an overwhelming desire to not only accept everything he said, but also a strong overwhelming desire to fall down on my face and worship him. And it was very evident that he promoted that desire, and that was my main reason for knowing he was an evil spirit sent by satan. For you see, for years I have been seeing in my studies and in communication with the Lord some things along the line of God's grace that I have not heard a whisper about from other sources. I have taught it some and have always received opposition every time I teach on it. And I really haven't matured to the point that I love all of the opposition that comes my way. So I was a prime candidate for such an experience.

This is what concerns me. In 2 Corinthians 11:13-15, it is plain that satan transforms himself (appearing to be) into an angel of light (which is Christ Himself). It seems obvious that some ministries today are used by the same demonic thrust. The appearance of Godlikeness is there, etc. However, some things satan and his false ministries cannot duplicate, the main one being God's love. God's love is a dimension about which satan knows nothing and it horrifies him and his kingdom. Also the fruits of the spirit cannot be duplicated by evil spirits. (See Galatians 5:22-23.)

These evil spirits do not do anything that they have not done for years. I see very clearly these spirits have crept into many religious circles. While certain religious groups would never admit their doctrine is to be worshipped, you will meet great opposition if you do not go along with their programs. In face of opposition, one can see that the fruits of the spirit are of less importance to them than their doctrine. One can test the spirit that motivates them by what comes out of their mouths and what kind of actions they promote in the face of opposition to their doctrines.

I also see people today in powerful positions or having great sums of money, both Christians and non, who seem to promote an atmosphere in which there is an indirect call for worship to be directed toward them. And there is that sense of giving them reverence, something that should only be given to God. Many say, "No, not me!" Then why do some give or do for people in those positions more than they would for someone who can do nothing more than thank them?

It was so obvious that a spirit of this nature was influencing as I tuned into a certain T.V. program where they were giving awards for best songs and singers of the year. I noticed a group that came in first place with their song and their singing. Throngs of people literally worshipped them. It was very obvious by the way the people responded to their group, etc. I want to make a statement and this statement is not critical, only observational. I looked at the group who came in first place across our nation and thought, "The only way I could enjoy this group's singing or even their presence is if I would numb my natural mind with drugs or something that would keep me from thinking clearly." I am not trying to be crude or critical; I am a very open-minded person. My point is this – evil spirits that desire human worship are very much in operation today, causing people to take on their demonic characteristics.

These spirits try to use all of us. But many people do not really believe this because they do not know the truth concerning the issue. These spirits are quite subtle. For example, they creep into our lives trying to make us desire the acclamation or reverence of others, with the train of thought being, "I am better than someone else." We need to have a good understanding of demons and their operations so we can stop them in their first stages of using us.

Just to give you a little more insight, I want to tell you of some other situations in which evil spirits are involved, though not so obviously. I first taught the Bible as a soldier boy at the age of 18 in Pusan, Korea in 1968. My wife and I pastored our first church in 1972 and have done nothing else but pastor since 1978 for our primary source of income, etc. Simply by studying over the years, as well as observing, we learned a few things. For example, I noticed over the years that some churches would know more about their hymn books than they did about the Bible.

You could see when a song was requested that they knew the exact page it was on. They also would not have to even turn to many of the songs as they knew them by heart. But if you would ask them to quote three verses out of the Bible verbatim, they could not nor could they tell you where a Scripture was located. And if you would happen to preach a message that would be contrary to their song-book, it would not make any difference how many verbatim Scriptures you had given in support of your point, you would be in big trouble. If your salary could have been determined after such a message, it would have been cut. It is beyond imagination what people will do to you if you persist in such messages.

The same thing can happen in organizations that have articles of incorporation which they believe carry more authenticity and weight than the Bible. The truth is, such people are worshipping "a knowledge" more than THE KNOWLEDGE OF THE LORD JESUS CHRIST. (See 2 Corinthians 10:3-5).

Too often people are being used by religious demons who will fight as far as possible to prove they are right. This spirit has crept into many churches and has kept God's fullness from being in operation. Yes, many churches and church leaders have organized the Holy Spirit right out of the church. And if we enter into such a setting, deliberately choosing to antagonize such people, then we are being used by an equally-evil spirit. As true followers of Christ, our intention must always be to bring joy and blessing to humanity and not to compromise because of religious spirits that demand worship.

Let us look at other Scriptures to support how satan and his kingdom are of the first heaven. Ephesians 3:10 plainly shows how the Holy Spirit is prompting the issue that we should know the intent of principalities and powers in heavenly places and that this wisdom may be known to the church. This passage is describing a kingdom, a heavenly sphere where demonic forces exist. The following Scriptures also confirm the existence of a heavenly sphere where demonic forces exist: 1 Kings 21:3-5; Daniel 4:26; Judges 5:20; Job 35:11; Isaiah 34:4; Jeremiah 8:2; Daniel 8:10; Zephaniah 1:5; Mark 13:25; Luke 21:26; Acts 4:42.

This sphere correlates totally and concisely with a kingdom and that kingdom would be of satan in the first heaven. So satan does have a kingdom; and it is in the first heaven.

CHAPTER 4

How Satan Operates

We have been looking at the origin of satan and his kingdom, but now I want to show you how they operate. Daniel 10 provides a clear picture of a double kingdom and also supports the teaching concerning the existence of a demonic kingdom. Some may think the location of satan's kingdom unimportant. But we need to know everything God wants us to know about satan and his kingdom. Why? Because both are very real and are eternal. They possess eternal damnation – they have been around a long time.

When discussing demons and satan, we are not dealing with some little figment of our imaginations. We are not teaching something only the illiterate or feebleminded believe; although that is exactly what satan wants people to think in order to keep intelligent believers from halting his manuevers. Satan and his own hate us, and their primary thrust is to destroy, kill and steal.

We need to beat them at their game, and we will. We are. Read the end of the book. Notice Revelation 12:11 in which we are told that a certain people will overcome satan by the Word of God and by the testimony of the Lord Jesus Christ. This is the only way to overcome satan. We have authority over him and his kingdom, but we must see the need to mature.

Resistance Must Be 100% –

When Jesus first appeared to me and told me that for the rest of my life I would be in confrontation with evil spirits, but that He would be with me, I learned that because of Jesus being with me, I had authority over the worst confrontation with satan. And for the first few years, when evil spirits would appear to me, I could easily discern what type of spirit they were, their motive and operation. Rarely would this confrontation last more than a couple of minutes. However, many times it seemed as long as 30 minutes. But that is the nature of torment in which sin, evil spirits and torment are co-equal terms. And torment always seems longer than it is.

But I noticed after a few years that these evil spirits were getting more hesitant about leaving when I would rebuke them. Then the torment of their presence increased to the point that a spirit would only tremble when I rebuked him in Jesus' name and would not leave. I desperately sought direction from the Holy Spirit. There was no audible voice or anything of that nature, but a very real perception, more sure than the earth's existence, came to me from the Holy Spirit saying: "Evil spirits know when we are 100 percent against their being in our presence. And if even one percent of our being doesn't mind their presence, they do not have to leave."

The Bible says in James 1:7,8, that a double-minded person will not receive from the Lord. You will find the same teaching in Matthew 6:22-24. Also by experience, you should know that if you have the slightest acceptance of giving into a temptation, that thought will stay. In fact, it will stay until you deal with removing it from your life with 100 percent of your determination. Of course that determination must be coming from a life that knows it has authority over evil spirits. And never forget, that is exactly what we are dealing with. Thoughts and temptations to sin are green lights in knowing a very real demonic, eternally-hellbound, evil spirit is present. And this is the devil's first step in causing a person to take on satanic characteristics.

Forever Growing and Changing –

Somone might ask, "Why did the evil spirits leave at first when you rebuked them and not later?" If you have ever noticed people when they are first born again, they begin to read their Bibles and in such simplicity they get their prayers answered. But as time goes on, their prayers are not always answered. They are doing everything the same; they haven't changed, but herein lies the problem. We need to be forever changing. If we are not changing, we are dying. Anything that doesn't grow is dying; something that grows is always changing. God wants us to grow spiritually.

"Now the Lord is that Spirit: and where the Spirit of the Lord is, there is liberty.

"But we all, with open face beholding as in a glass the glory of the Lord, are changed into the same image from glory to glory, even as by the Spirit of the Lord," (2 Corinthians 3:17,18).

Here we are plainly taught that we are changed by continually looking to the Word of God. God will honor us at the level of our knowledge and understanding, but He expects us to walk in that light which we have.

"This then is the message which we have heard of him, and declare unto you, that God is light, and in him is no darkness at all.

"If we say that we have fellowship with him, and walk

in darkness, we lie, and do not the truth:

"But if we walk in the light, as he is in the light, we have fellowship one with another, and the blood of Jesus Christ his Son cleanseth us from all sin," (1 John 1:5-7).

No one will ever be able to get me to believe that God is not a God of love – love beyond our understanding. But if I would give my children the same food that I did when they were babies, I would be evil. Likewise, God loves us so much that He wants us to mature for our benefit.

We need to be sure we have been born again and are filled with the Spirit of God so we can have deeper insights into God's Word and the realm of the spirit. If you are mature in the Lord, you can know there are more demons assigned to you than the person who knows little or nothing about the things of God. To whom much is given much is required.

We must get serious with God. Do not accept this out of fear. We should want to just grow closer to God. He has a banquet table spread for us, and we are over here eating cheese and crackers. God has so much more for us. He isn't trying to get us into a religious bondage. He has divine, sublime joy for us in greater and greater depths that require growth on our parts before we can experience them.

Don't Play With Sin –

I have lost two very dear people in my life, and the destruction of both was of satan. I could have stopped it from happening, but I wasn't acting on the full knowledge that I possessed. So the author of their destrcution was satan.

In 1976, my wife and I had been pastoring churches and evangelizing for a few years. We owned a new car, new truck, a fairly-new home, and our own business. From the outside, things were looking fine. But I was living beneath my privileges in God and the revelations He had given me. Actually, I was afraid to trust God to help me do what He had asked me to. This also led to allowing things into my life, as a minister, that weren't God ordained.

"When the unclean spirit is gone out of a man, he walketh through dry places, seeking rest, and findeth none.

"Then he saith, I will return into my house from whence I came out; and when he is come, he findeth it empty, swept, and garnished.

"Then goeth he, and taketh with himself seven other spirits more wicked than himself, and they enter in and dwell there: and the last state of that man is worse than the first. Even so shall it be also unto this wicked generation," (Matthew 12:43-35).

This Scripture teaches us that if we let one evil sprit into our life, he will bring seven more in who are worse than he. If you play with a little something that is not God ordained, you are playing with an evil spirit that will do his best to take you to the next step of having even more evil in your life. It's the little foxes that spoil the vine.

I stood outside the delivery room and watched my wife for several hours being tortured by difficult labor in the delivery of our baby. The doctor reported a possibility of my losing her; the baby did die. It was like watching someone you love in hell. As I watched and heard the screams and moans for hours through the small delivery room window, it seemed as though she was in a torture chamber.

Things will happen because we are not where we ought to be. God has a road for us and it is a road of protection; but if we walk down the devil's road, even though it's a little close and we know better, we are open game for the devil. I promise you one thing, the devil will take the thing you love most and will show no mercy. As never before, this is a truth we had better grasp. Satan knows he has but a little time, and he is exercising great wrath THAT THE WORLD HAS NEVER KNOWN ANYTHING ABOUT. I want you to understand, you are no match for him outside of God. The devil shakes kingdoms, the earth and cities. We are no match for him without God.

The Double Kingdom –

If you read the whole chapter of Daniel 10, you will find that there is a double kingdom here – natural and spiritual. Earlier we looked at Ezekiel 28 and it too displays in simplicity a double kingdom. It talks about a spiritual and a natural being. What takes place on this earth first takes place in the atmospheric heaven just like in Tyrus. This is the reason we need to know about satan's kingdom; so when we perceive what is going on there, we can stop it before it happens in this natural world. Every evil thing that has ever happened or will happen, first occurred in the first heaven.

This particular time of Ezekiel 28 refers to satan himself, prince of Tyrus. And then there was a natural prince. Devils will make you what they are. A lying devil will make you a liar. Devils of adultery, gossip and religion will make you what they are. One of a demon's primary goals is to embody a human being because he can express himself to the fullest extent through a human being. If they can't get a human being, they will go through animals.

We find that when Jesus cast the demons out of the swine, their greatest concern was having no where to go, no human through which to work. I'll tell you who demons really like – someone who claims to be a Christian. Such a person is not necessarily demon possessed. Rather, they are just being used to stop the will of God from being done in this earth. Remember, one of Jesus' right-hand

38

men was being used by satan himself to try to stop the will of God from being accomplished in this earth.

Christians Can Be Used By Satan –

That is the reason we cannot be moved when the Spirit of God deals with us about something, and it is sound in the Word of God. Satan will use the best Christians in whom you have the most confidence to get you out of the will of God. Christians cannot be demon possessed in their spirits, but THEY CAN BE AND ARE USED by evil spirits.

Have you ever known a Christian who was always displaying doubt in their words and actions everytime you saw them? The Bible calls doubt an evil spirit. Their philosophy is that God will do it for someone else but not me. Every time you see such Christians, they are sick. Still others may always be stealing. Malachi 3:8-10 says that those who do not pay their tithes are stealing from God. Anybody who will steal from God cannot be trusted. They will steal from anyone; they are dishonest.

"Then I lifted up mine eyes, and looked, and behold, a certain man clothed in linen, whose loins were girded with fine gold of Uphaz:

"His body also was like the beryl, and his face as the appearance of lightning, and his eyes as lamps of fire, and his arms and his feet like in colour to polished brass, and the voice of his words like the voice of a multitude," (Daniel 10:5,6).

Immediately we begin to see that this isn't a natural being. We can also see that no one in the natural looks like or is described like this. This is definitely the description of a spiritual being. The next verse says:

"And I Daniel alone saw the vision: for the men that were with me saw not the vision; but a great quaking fell

upon them, so that they fled to hide themselves.

"Therefore I was left alone, and saw this great vision, and there remained no strength in me: for my comeliness was turned in me into corruption, and I retained no strength.

"Yet heard I the voice of his words: and when I heard the voice of his words, then was I in a deep sleep on my face, and my face toward the ground.

"And behold, an hand touched me, which set me upon my knees and upon the palms of my hands," (Daniel 5:7-10).

Mental Telepathy Or God? –

I want to stop here and deviate just a little bit because I want to talk about a demon that tries to get in the Charismatic circles. It really is a spirit of mental telepathy. Part of this spirit's promotion is emotionalism and it thrives on people falling down as if by God. If the Spirit of God comes on you, there are times when you will fall down. I know that it is something that many Charismatic and Full-Gospel people idolize: but nevertheless, some truth needs to be mentioned here.

Have you ever noticed there is more excitement about people falling down than there is about the eternal Word of God? Have you ever noticed that they always fall backwards? Study your Bibles again and notice how people fell when the Spirit of God moved upon them in that fashion. I am quite comfortable in saying that if you can find where even 20 percent of the time people of the Bible fell backwards, you would be doing good. That means that at least 80 percent fell another way – and that way was on their faces or forward. I am not criticizing the manifestations of God, as I have seen people fall backwards under the power of God on concrete with no catchers and no trying to catch themselves in the least; and there was no harm to their person whatsoever. In fact, if God had not been moving them, they would have been badly hurt. And I can go on and on with such stories.

But notice something else here in the Daniel 10 text. Not only did Daniel fall on his face, but the Spirit of God touched him again and popped him back up on his hands and knees. Now I have seen people fall, but I have never seen them pop back up. We will know the Spirit of God is in operation when things of this nature happen. We need to make sure we do not get into sensationalism. I myself have fallen by supernatural manifestations. However, I do not approve of "pushy" preachers who try to help God out. In other words, when people fall sick and get up sick, maybe it wasn't God. Maybe it was a sensational experience. I know personally a very intelligent lady who fell as she was pressured and hit her head on the back of a pew. She had to be hospitalized for a great length of time for a severely damaged skull.

God is not into anything which would cause people harm. Our churches should stand on the Word of God as final authority and then fewer people would be falling under false influences, physically and spiritually. We need to have more of God's manifestations, not less; but they need to be God initiated, not manmade. Such will come about when we do what Jeremiah says in Chapter 33, Verse 3 (which we quoted earlier).

If God is really present and the proof is people falling down, then that means He is present. However, if His presence is truly there, other manifestations will also be evident, such as blinded eyes being opened; *people without limbs receiving new ones;* the dead being raised, etc.

God wants the supernatural to be evidenced in such astonishing ways that His holiness will receive full attention. In fact I know that if we neglect supernatural miracles in the realm of the senses, as well as in the realm of the imagination, miracles that confirm the atoning work of the Lord Jesus Christ, there will be no rapture. I am only saying these things, not to destroy your believing in the supernatural, but just to keep it on sound Scriptural track.

Keeping this last statement in mind let me deal with some other obvious, erroneous problems. Again this issue is nothing more than a spirit of mental telepathy. Let me explain how a spirit of mental telepathy operates. A person who is used by this spirit will instruct by words, trains of thought, body language, etc. as to what they want their followers to know or do. At the highest order or most mature level, they will instruct with their minds only. Their followers will follow their desires. When one is used by a spirit of any kind, the first obvious desire is to draw attention to themselves. You can also notice by close observation that the tenderness of God's goodness is not seen. Another manifestation of this false spirit that occurs today is the "blowing" ministry. There is one verse in the Bible that talks about Jesus blowing on his disciples to receive the Holy Spirit. It is in the Bible but any time someone builds a ministry on any manifestation, I believe there is a problem.

Again with the love of God in my heart, I want to say we are not to be critical of a person because this is a deceiving spirit itself. I believe the Spirit of God might do this occasionally; but if He does, there should be manifestations other than people falling down. What about those people without limbs? I believe we get into problems any time we put more prominence over any one thing other than the riches of God's goodness. I am simply grieved that satan's sly, cunning devices have kept God's people from enjoying God's richest and best.

In Matthew 24:4, Jesus said the very first evil spirit of the last days would be a spirit of DECEPTION, and you will notice this spirit of the end time will be the leading, prominent spirit. Please understand that this deception is my main concern – not to criticize, slam or shame anyone. And I ask you to please do the same. We only need be aware of the tricks of the devil and avoid being used by yet another evil spirit in finding fault with another person.

Galatians 6:1,2, says when we who are spiritual see one with a fault, we are to RESTORE SUCH A ONE BACK TO CHRIST. We need to understand that for everything God has, satan has a counterfeit. Some will say the Lord has revealed a person's fault to them. I would like to say that if someone does anything other than that which would promote such a one back to the Lord, they did not get that information from the Lord. Because if they did, all they would want to do is keep the information to themselves and God, because of the holiness of Him who is confiding such information. I know this has been joked about, but it is very real and true – God's gift of the word of knowledge discloses or reveals secrets and satan's counterfeit gift IS THE GIFT OF SUSPICION.

Let's get back on course. In the above-mentioned passage in Daniel, Verse 10-21, we can see that a supernatural, spiritual being communicated with Daniel. Both Daniel and this being warred against a spiritual prince of Persia and Grecia. Again, we see a double kingdom. And again, we see clearly a first heavenly kingdom of evil residing over an earthly kingdom, making the earthly what it was. Ezekiel 28 also gives a clear picture of this double kingdom. So what we need to know is when we see something contrary in lives or a situation in this natural world, do not treat it as the "source" of the problem; instead, we

43

must deal with the true source of trouble.

For example, if we sit in a church and continually see doubt and unbelief spoken and practiced, we need to get into a private place of prayer and cast down, stop, in Jesus' Name and rebuke the manuevers of those evil spirits who are above that situation.

"Wherefore God also hath highly exalted him, and given him a name which is above every name:" (Philippians 2:9).

CHAPTER 5

Obvious Manifestations of Satan

Satan can take advantage of us if we're ignorant of his devices. In 2 Corinthians 2:11, we are told not to be ignorant of the devices of the devil. If we are ignorant of his maneuvers, manipulations, the order of his manifestations and the order of his operation, we will be defeated. So we are going to be dealing with the obvious manifestations of satan in this chapter.

We can see from Scripture how satan and his demons are in full operation. I want to expose their operations. Many Americans are guilty of thinking they are too intelligent to believe in satan, and so they try to deal with the operations of demons and satan by using natural or mental solutions instead of dealing with them supernaturally. Satan and demons are a spiritual problem, not a natural or mental problem.

People who try to deal with demons and satan with psychological or natural solutions, experience great failure. This is why so many psychiatrists who do not believe in satan or demon spirits have such mental problems or breakdowns themselves. Many become suicidal. In fact, in my observation and study over the years, I have found that psychiatrists lead all professions in mental break-downs and suicide. Again, this is because too many psychiatrists treat spiritual problems with carnal, natural methods. To deal with spiritual problems, a person must be at least born again or they are useless against demonic powers.

Obvious Manifestations –

Let's look at obvious satanic manifestations. Mark 5:1-5 states:

"And they came over unto the other side of the sea, into the country of the Gadarenes.

"And when he was come out of the ship, immediately there met him out of the tombs a man with an unclean spirit.

"Who had his dwelling among the tombs; and no man could bind him, no, not with chains:

"Because that he had been often bound with fetters and chains, and the chains had been plucked asunder by him, and the fetters broken in pieces: neither could any man tame him.

"And always, night and day, he was in the mountains, and in the tombs, crying, and cutting himself with stones."

Obviously a demon spirit was possessing this man. Even someone who didn't believe in demon spirits would have to see that something supernatural was controlling this man, because the Bible shows that he possessed supernatural strength when it describes how no fetters nor chains could hold him. He could break the fetters into pieces; and it says that no man could tame him. Well, you can obviously see that such behavior would require supernatural strength. If you read the entire chapter and observe the nature, make-up and character of this individual who had the legion of demons in him, it becomes obvious that his strength came from supernatural manifestations of demonic spirits within him.

"And there were seven sons of one Sceva, a Jew, and chief of the priests, which did so.

"And the evil spirit answered and said, Jesus, and Paul I know; but who are ye?

"And the man in whom the evil spirit was leaped on them, and overcame them, and prevailed against them, so that they fled out of that house naked and wounded," (Acts 19:14-16).

Here's something else I want you to see. There were seven natural men, seven sons of Sceva, along with one individual. And the Bible says this individual had an evil spirit; therefore, an evil spirit dwelt within him. However, someone who did not even believe in the Bible would have to know something was obviously very wrong with this individual, something supernaturally evil about him. Notice the incredible strength that enabled him to overcome seven men. Again, you see the evil and supernatural strength of this individual would have to be demonic in origin.

"And it came to pass, as we went to prayer, a certain damsel possessed with a spirit of divination met us, which brought her masters much gain by soothsaying:

"The same followed Paul and us, and cried, saying, These men are the servants of the most high God, which shew unto us the way of salvation," (Acts 16:16,17).

Here we find that the Apostle Paul was in the city of Philippi, and his purpose was to promote and preach the Gospel. Present in his company was a damsel who had an evil spirit of divination. There was a great deal of harassment because of the way she followed the Apostle Paul and so forth. Several days passed before finally the Apostle Paul turned and cast the spirit out of her. This damsel clearly possessed supernatural abilities that were not of God.

Satan is a supernatural being just as God is supernatural. Supernatural in these situations? Yes. Of God? No! This was obviously a supernatural manifestation situation because of the woman's abilities to tell fortunes, etc. She had an evil spirit of divination. But from the natural standpoint, people clearly saw the supernatural abilities. Here again, we are observing an evil spirit in action since no glory was given to God. Also such practices have no Scriptural basis. Any time soothsaying and divination are in manifestation, God gets no glory; there are no sound Scriptures to support the manifestation; fear is known; and an eerie atmosphere prevails. The Bible says we can know the truths by the fruits. (See Galatians 5:22,23, and keep in mind that the "faith" discusssed in this passage refers to faithfulness to God and His holy Word.)

Another passage of Scripture in which we see the involvement of an evil spirit is 1 Samuel 28:8-16. Here we find the story of Saul when he came by night to see a woman who had a familiar spirit. Anytime you have to sneak around to do something, you can rest assured an evil spirit is involved. Jesus was our perfect example. He said in Mark 14, and I paraphrase, "...I taught, lived and did everything that heaven stands for openly among you, but now you sneak in the night to do evil to me, to take me to be crucified!"

That is exactly how the devil and his bunch still operate today. Satan and his demons like to crucify people today by destroying their character with words. Sneaking around with evil words will take you to an evil experience!

Yes, Saul sought evil counsel by night, and asked the woman if she would call Samuel from the dead, sort of a seance. The Bible says in this particular chapter that the woman worked with familiar spirits and was a wizard. It also makes note of her being a witch. (This you can notice in the footnotes of many Bibles.) So apparently this

48

woman would call people up from the dead. People of this calibre communicate with evil, familiar spirits. Saul had a lot of problems in his life, and Samuel was a prominent prophet of God in his day. He was known to give inspiration and direction from God to His people. Saul wanted, not repentance, but just some supernatural direction. And he thought since Samuel was used of God when he was alive that maybe he could help him now. Instead of seeking God himself, Saul sought for a wizard, a clairvoyant, one who works with familiar spirits. He asked her to bring Samuel, who had been dead for quite some time, from the dead.

And she did; but of course, it was not Samuel who appeared. It was, instead, a spirit that had followed Samuel. As you study the Bible, you will find that familiar spirits follow all of us. They can intimidate us as far as representing us in a bad way, because they follow us and gain familiar information about us. They know all about us so they can duplicate our knowledge to a degree by listening to what we say, watching our habits, etc. Then they can manifest things about us because they are very familiar with us. That is the reason the Bible calls them familiar spirits. They mimic us.

And that is what took place in this passage. A familiar (mimicking) spirit, who had been familiar with Samuel, appeared. A person in the natural can know when manifestations of an evil spirit are occurring because an evil spirit will bring fear. Fear is promoted in an atmosphere of this nature. There is no glorification to God, no Scriptural settings for it, etc.

Today in our world, there are churches that deal with familiar spirits. Many of them will use the Bible, the same King James Bible that we use. They will have services where a medium or a clairvoyant will, in essence, fall into a trance and call up people from the dead. That is what they say is happening. Actually what really is taking place is there is a manifestation of a familiar spirit. These spirits will come up out of the floor, fly around the room, make objects move and other quite obvious supernatural manifestations. Many people today are being mislead because of the supernatural aura of it all. Yes – supernatural. Of God? No! So this would also be another obvious manifestation of satan.

Looking at our day and time, we can see many obvious manifestations of satan. Notice people in mental institutions who have incredible strength. It is quite obvious. You can see the gleam in their eyes, the evilness of their person, etc. Yes, there are people in our day who are embodied by evil spirits. Notice the nature of those involved in fortune telling – their office, its location, the anti-christ, anti-bible presentation of it all. Quite obviously these people are involved in the evil supernatural and they are under the influence of evil spirits.

CHAPTER 6

Not-So-Obvious
Manifestations of Satan

I am extremely convinced that there will be no rapture if the church neglects the ministry of supernatural signs in the realm of the senses and the imagination with the purpose of confirming the atoning work of the Lord Jesus Christ. Someday I hope to write a book giving much evidence and simplicity to this subject, but I must stay on course with the present topic.

In the last days there will be "lying, supernatural signs, wonders and power." Jesus said in Matthew 7:20-27, that there would be many that will say, "Lord, have we not prophesied in thy name (supernatural utterance concerning secrets); cast out devils in thy name (the appearance of supernatural power); and appearance of wonderful words (supernatural miracles in the senses and imagination realm)?" But Jesus said that He will say, "Depart from me for I never knew you." So in the last days there will obviously be the evil, supernatural manifestations. But we must focus our attention on the will of God and not neglect the ministry of true, God-ordained supernatural signs and wonders.

However, a great deal of the supernatural works will

be of satan; and the only people who will know the difference will be the diligent, spirit and Bible-filled believers who walk in God's love. Jesus also said we could know the difference between good and evil by their fruits, not by signs and wonders, etc. I believe and practice speaking in tongues on a daily basis, but tongues is not the final proof of being Holy-Spirit filled. Number One, holiness is proof of the Holy Spirit's indwelling or evidence that He possesses a person. Other sound, Scriptural proof would be LOVE, JOY, PEACE, LONGSUFFERING, GENTLENESS, GOODNESS, FAITHFULNESS TO GOD AND HIS WORD, MEEKNESS AND TEMPERANCE. (See Galatians 5:22,23.)

Of God or Of Satan? –

Yes, in the last days there will be two categories of obvious supernatural manifestations: one of God and one of satan. And in the category of satan one group will have never known God. (See Matthew 7:21.) And then there will be those who are more zealous for the signs and wonders than they are for the fruit of the Holy Spirit. These too will fall into satan's trap.

The Bible plainly teaches us in James 2:19, "Thou believest that there is one God; thou doest well: the devils also believe, and tremble."

When you begin to know the Word of God and use it, the devil and his demons are horrified and tremble. When Jesus appeared to me back in October of 1973, and told me that for the rest of my life I would encounter demon forces, He also said I would literally see, hear, smell and feel them in the realm of the spirit. Since then, such events have occurred many times. In this chapter we will share a few of these experiences only for the purpose of giving us greater understanding in illustrating the truths of God's Word.

We have been delivered out of the kingdom of darkness, and if we are not in the kingdom of God, we are in the kingdom of darkness. IF WE ARE NOT UNDER THE INFLUENCE OF GOD'S KINGDOM, WE ARE UNDER THE INFLUENCE OF THE DEVIL'S KINGDOM. Whether we want to believe it or not and whether the world wants to believe it or not, it is true. The more I study the Bible the more I see that either you are walking in the Spirit or you are under the influence of demonic powers – one of the two. I used to think, "Well, there is the realm of God that influences us or we are influenced by carnality, or by demonic powers." But the more I study the Bible, the more I find that carnality is a tool of the demonic realm. Romans 8:7, says carnality is enmity against God. If anything is against God, it is of the kingdom of darkness. The word "enmity" also means enemy. So as satan is the enemy of God, so is everything that is against God of the kingdom of satan. We are influenced by God or we are influenced by the devil. Yes, even Christians.

I did not say Christians are demon possessed, just that some of them are more influenced by satan than they are of God. And this is why the CHURCH has seen very little of what God wants, accomplished in the world. Psalms 78:41, says it was God's people who "limited the Holy One of Israel." It was God's people who prevented God from doing what He fully desired to do for His people.

2 Chronicles 7:14, says, *"If my people which are called by my name, shall humble themselves, and pray, and seek my face and turn from their wicked ways; then will I hear from heaven, and will forgive their sin, and will heal their land."*

Note, God did not say, "If the world or the sinners clean up their acts." Rather, He was talking to His own people. We can see this same thought in James 4:8, where we are told to "Draw nigh to God, and He will draw nigh to you...." The real problem is God's people today are not as serious with God as they need to be. They are being used of the devil and will physically fight you or take you to court to sue you to prove that they are not being used of the devil. James 3:10, basically cautions that out of the same person cannot proceed manifestations of the devil and the next moment manifestations from God. The church needs to find the little foxes who are spoiling the vines – the little invisible demons that are keeping the church lame, such as idle, unprofitable, useless and foolish words.

Many Christians live and die, being used by evil spirits. Yes, they go on to heaven, but what a second-rate way of living! What a cheated life style! I would rather be influenced by goodness, joy, peace and God. Yes, we are influenced by one of the two. There is only one sin that takes you to hell, and that is rejecting Jesus Christ as Lord. Nothing else will take you to hell. The other sins will allow you to have some hell on earth, as the wages of all sin is some type of death.

We need to understand that all sin is a seed and when a seed is fully matured, it will express and exhibit what its parent is. Satan is the father of all sin, and WHEN ALL SIN IS FULLY MATURED,IT WILL TAKE ONE TO HELL. So if one is not influenced by God, then he is influenced by satan. If influenced by satan, the ultimate maturity leads one to an eternal hell. That is the ultimate goal of all evil spirits and what they want to express in the lives of humanity.

Faults Or Demons? –

Many Christians have what they call faults, which they blame on their heritage, etc. However, it is nothing more than them giving into an evil spirit. I have used the same excuse for years. I used to say that it was because of my heritage of strong Irish and strong American Indian that I have such a bad temper. But I didn't get it from Ireland nor from the Indians. I got it from hell. And when I humbled myself to accept that it was an evil spirit that was using me, I fought it with the Word of God. I have been reprogrammed. Anyone who remotely knows me, knows that I am not a person with a bad or any temper. My Father which art in heaven, who walks with me, doesn't have a temper, and I am LEARNING to be just like Him. He's gentle, kind and longsuffering. I have a new heritage; I have a new Father. But I want you to know that the demon of anger used to use me. And he tries to come back occasionally, only to find there is no room in the life he used to live in. It is too full of light for darkness to enter.

And even as a minister of the Gospel, I have sat under the best ministries of our day AND CRITICIZED them (maybe only to myself and to my wife); but nevertheless, I was entertaining a spirit of criticism. I had to repent if I wanted God's best. That is a big reason why so many of God's people have second best in life; they would rather suffer than crucify the flesh and pride to say, "I WAS WRONG. AN EVIL SPIRIT USED ME." If we start understanding that what some say is just a little habit, is really an evil spirit, then we will fight those habits as we would fight what we believe to be major sins. Why? Because we will realize we are dealing with an actual demon.

A demon's name will reveal what he is. A demon of criticism will make you a critical person. A lying demon will make you a liar. Demons will express through you what they are and they will try to make you what they are.

We need to fight these spirits as never before as the time is short. Maybe you will go to heaven even though you are used by a spirit of gluttony or worry, for example. But what about the ones you love so dearly who are going to spend eternity in a tormenting hell because you haven't enough of God in you to stop the powers of satan from controlling those you love? All sin is selfish. No one ever commits adultery for someone else's benefit; and it is just as stupid to say you committed any kind of sin for someone else.

Another reason we need to fight these spirits is because they do not stop; they grow. And they let in other spirits worse than themselves. Look at this example: a demon of worry lets in a spirit of doubt; and he grows to the point that you doubt that God's Word is true. Such as, "Oh, dear God, I can't meet all of my bills." Then what they are really saying is the God of all creation isn't what He said He is, that He cannot do what He said He would do. Really what has occurred is that they have grown so demonically bold they are calling God a liar. Notice the Book of Numbers, Chapter 13 and Hebrews 3, where the Bible calls attention to the fact that doubting is evil. It is an evil spirit.

Many doubting Christians will say, "Well, I just cannot stop it." That is the same thing an alcoholic or dope addict says. I just cannot stop it. It's a demon power, and we better learn to fight these sort of things with the same thrust that we would a demon spirit.

Discerning And The Five Senses –

Primarily what I want us to understand is that just because it doesn't seem obvious, doesn't mean no evil spirit is involved. It is very obvious when you have had an experience such as I have when satan himself walks into the room where you are. He looked just as real as anybody, though at times I knew if I were to try to touch him, I could not because I realized he was a spirit. There are times when I do feel in the realm of the spirit and know it is only a spirit image standing in front of me. If I were to try to touch them, my hand would go through them. When I first started having these appearances there would be times when I would wake during the night session because of a perception that someone was in my room. I would get out of bed with the intention of defending my home and would begin swinging my fists at demons, only to see and hear them laugh. My hands were going through their being to no avail.

This is only one type of manifestation of the gift of discerning spirits. The gift of discerning spirits will give you the ability to EXERCISE IN THE SPIRIT all of the five physical senses. In essence it seems like your five physical senses are in operation at different times, but it is your five spiritual senses. There are times when you will only see, hear, feel, touch or taste. Many times in church settings I will only see a spirit; such as the time when I was preaching and saw a spirit that was about the size of a man's hand, attached to an older woman's neck and right shoulder area. It had legs about eight inches long that went down the front of her chest and legs that went down her back about the same length. I stopped preaching and told the lady I wanted to deal with the problem in that area of her body. As I cursed the problem, the spirit fell to the ground and went out of the building and down the street. (Since many times people who do not understand the teaching on demons, will become upset if I actually use the word, I usually just call it a problem, even though I am actually dealing with a demonic spirit.)

Anyway, as the demon fell, the lady stood and began to praise God audibly and emotionally. Then several people began to do the same thing. I thought it was rather strange for people to act so emotional, only to find out after the service that a few months earlier, the lady had had a stroke on that side of her neck, leaving her without the ability to speak.

Another situation comes to mind that helps us understand the gift of discerning of spirits in which one or more of the senses are used. I can never recall up to this time having had an experience in which all five senses were in operation. It does seem as I grow in the Lord that more of the senses come into operation. But I remember just about three years ago, a man had a backache. When I laid my hand on the area of his back which he said had been aching, I felt a spirit about ten inches long that was attached flat against the side of his back. Actually it felt like a large leech or snake-type of thing without being slimy. I rebuked it, and it slowly began to move down his back just as he was saying the pain was moving down his back. After a short time, I saw the demon drop from the man's hip area onto the floor and go out the building towards the southwest door. As the spirit left, so did the pain – 100 percent. So you can see from the first story how only seeing was manifested and in the second, the sense of touch.

We must understand that satan's kingdom is very real and extremely active today. As we are keenly aware of their presence and purposes, we can discern demons and cast them out of situations. The not-so-obvious demon spirits are actually the ones that are doing the most destructive work today, especially in the church.

Ways To Deal With Demonic Spirits –

In dealing with spirits, I find that different spirits have to be dealt with in various ways. The best way to rebuke certain demons is to simply ignore them. For example, once when Jesus' life was in jeopardy, He walked through the midst of the crowd, knowing that no man could take his life. He simply ignored the threats against Him, and no harm came to him. Colossians 2:15, also verifies this point:

"And having spoiled principalities and powers, he

made a shew of them openly, triumphing over them in it."

Notice the above Scripture says that principalities and powers have been spoiled. In the Greek, the word "spoiled" parallels the word "paralyzed," meaning "put to nought or nothing." So the best way to treat a principality that is paralyzed but is speaking threats, is to ignore it.

For example, when someone is being used by a spirit of anger, simply ignore them and leave their presence. I have tried to reason too many times with people under the influence of a demon of anger, and it doesn't work; because a spirit of anger will always bring AFTER HIM a spirit of unreasonableness. Such people will never reason with you. I have even tried agreeing with them and they will get mad at you for agreeing with them. Or else they will take a stand for what they were just previously against. But the way to stop (rebuke) that kind of a spirit is to ignore it. I'm telling you, if you don't, after a spirit of unreasonableness will come a spirit of strife and then violence. And if you are out of the will of God, you will be hurt physically, mentally and spiritually. And you are out of the will of God if you try to deal in any way with an angry spirit. Just ignore such spirits.

Notice how Jesus dealt with a spirit of false accusation in Isaiah 53: "He opened not His mouth." We always want to justify ourselves. And that is a good sign of selfishness, because self doesn't want to look bad, especially when we are not wrong! But you cannot receive any stronger false accusations than those Jesus received; and He stopped (rebuked) the evil spirit that tried to hinder the perfect plan of God by ignoring it. He opened not his mouth in Verse 7 of Isaiah 53.

Let me deviate just one moment to say this: if you are to ever do anything for God, you had better learn that the only way to get rid of a spirit of false accusation is to ignore it. Otherwise, you could be destroyed by that spirit.

59

And if you do not know how to stop it, you will never do much at all for the kingdom of God. As you grow in the Lord, you will receive direction from Him as to how to deal with different spirits.

There are tormenting spirits that are assigned primarily to attack the thought life. The way to deal with these spirits is to keep your mind stayed on things that are in agreement with God's Word or keep your mind filled with the Word of God itself. Let's look again at Matthew 12:43, where Jesus said, "When the unclean spirit is gone out of a man, he walketh through dry places, seeking rest, and findeth none." When this happens, the spirit will come back and try to regain entrance into that life. It looks in and sees the life is clean, garnished, swept and empty. The spirit then comes back in and brings seven more demons with it, and the poor man's state is worse now than at first.

Demons bring torment. One demon brings plenty, so you can see things are not pleasant for someone who has seven faults (demons) in their life. But here is the secret. There is nothing more powerful or more cleansing than the Word of God. So when, by the Word of God, we get these problems (spirits) out of our lives, we must make sure our lives are full of the Word so that when they come back, we will not be empty. And according to the Word of God, they will try to come back! If you have had a problem with worry, you sure do not need to be seven times worse off.

I lived in a particular home in my teenage years and have not been in it since 1977. However, because I lived there for several years, I could be blindfolded and still find the front or back doors. I could find every window, blindfolded. I would know my way around inside the house because I have lived there.

By the same token, you had better know if a spirit has ever lived in your life, because he can get back in so easily unless the powerful force of God's Word is filling your life. Such spirits would become familiar spirits because they would be very familiar with your life. Make sure when these spirits come, knock on the door and look into the small hidden window that nobody knows about other than someone who has lived there, that they not see only a clean, empty room. But may we also hear them say, "Oh, me, I've got to get away from here! It is full of light! Full of power, glory and holiness; SO FULL OF THE WORD OF GOD there is no room for me in there! I must leave at once!" This is one reason why Romans 12, says to be renewed in your mind by the Word of God.

How Demonic Spirits Get In –

Demons do not come rushing into our lives like a big storm. No, they are cunning. They creep in, in ways we think are so small and insignificant. Look at James 1:14:

"But every man is tempted, when he is drawn away of his own lust, and enticed."

First there is lust. Stop and think what lust is. Lust is only a thought. It is not the physical realm. It is thoughts injected such as, "Wouldn't you like to have that? Wouldn't you like to do that? Wouldn't you like to go there?" It is a thought. So every person is tempted when he is drawn away of his own lust. Here is something else I want you to see which coincides with what we are talking about.

"For we wrestle not against flesh and blood, but against principalities, against powers, against the rulers of the darkness of this world, against spiritual wickedness in high places," (Ephesians 6:12).

This Scripture plainly talks about four major orders of evil spirits; therefore, we can see there is organization in the demonic kingdom. So you can understand why James said, "If you allow first a spirit of lust in your life, he will open the door for the second order of demons in your life which will, in turn, take you into stronger torment, because they are more powerful. First lust; then lust allows enticement. Then when lust hath conceived, it bringeth forth sin; and when sin is finished with you, it bringeth forth death."

The order of progression is easily seen here in James. This is exactly how the kingdom of darkness operates. They first creep into our lives with things that SEEM to be so silly to most Christians, much less the world. People will even laugh at you when you try to point out that the first step is demonic, like you are a weird, narrow-minded bigot. And that is right, to a degree. We had better be narrow-minded about God's Word today or we will experience the devil's wages (Romans 6:23) which is death.

Yes, it seems like it wouldn't hurt anything to just have a little social drink. After all, we are of a more superior race and era of intelligence, so says a spirit of modern age, which is an age-old demonic lie that the demonic world has been using since the Garden of Eden. Look at Genesis 3:4, where the serpent is telling Eve that surely something so small and luscious as that fruit would not make her die. Surely she wouldn't die!

"There is a way which seemeth right unto a man, but the end thereof are the ways of death," (Proverbs 14:12).

We had better not go by what seems right; better to go by what the Bible says. There have been many good Christian people who have played with the devil and ended up in great torment and destruction. Maybe they started out socially drinking but ended up losing everything and becoming an alcoholic, dying with liver disease. I have seen preachers who thought it was okay to watch certain films in the privacy of their homes, just the wife and husband, end up down the road in divorce, losing their family, ministry and purpose of life.

We need to understand that just because a demon is not so obvious (or big) he, nonetheless, is still of the same kingdom of darkness that has a plan of torment and destruction for your life. His goal is to take you to death, spiritual death, eternal separation from God. That's their motive from the start, their goal, their vision of accomplishment for you, their plan that is as old as the world itself. Take your stand. If something is not of God, it is of satan. Your life depends on it.

We must learn to discern less-obvious demons and cast them out of our lives. We must never think we have arrived or matured to such a point that evil spirits cannot use us. Remember, Peter was used of satan himself; and Jesus turned to him and said, "Satan, get behind me."

"Wherefore let him that thinketh he standeth take heed lest he fall," (1 Corinthians 10:12).

Let them who think they are too mature in the Lord to make a mistake take heed lest they fall.

As long as we live on this earth we are on a battlefield and we had better stay on guard! Again, many will say this type of teaching is silly, only for the narrow-minded; and again I want to say what Isaiah says (and I paraphrase), "Perfect peace (the highest order of maturity) comes to those whose mind is stayed (focused) on the things of God, things that give Him glory and honor."

The word "peace" also means happiness, favor, rest, health and financial prosperity. So to allow one's mind to be narrowed or focused on God is life at its best, and to fail to do this is to experience torment and death. The decision is yours, not God's.

Laziness is a spirit. If we have a spirit of laziness, it will creep into our spiritual lives to where we are too lazy to go to church, too lazy to read our Bibles, too lazy to pray. Spirits will not stop until they have full control. It may take some time, maybe years, but they are persistent and will not give up. You have everything to lose; they have nothing! Why yield to torment? I'd rather yield to goodness, joy, happiness, life at its best!

63

There are born-again, Bible-carrying, tongue-talking Christians who are sometimes used in the gifts of the Holy Spirit. But the world says they have a chip on their shoulder. That's the world's analogy. But what is really wrong with them is they have a pet demon they have been carrying around for years. Everyone knows you had better watch everything you say around them, because they stay ready to bite at you like a mean Doberman dog. Here's what I want you to see: yes, they are going to heaven and are helping people. But just a little sin brings torment. You cannot be used, even by a little demon, and have all that God wants for you.

We need to know that there are microscopic demons. In Genesis 1:26, the Bible says God gave Adam dominion over every creeping thing that creepeth upon the earth. The words, "creepeth" and "creeping" in the Hebrew mean something that crawls or moves with short steps, by analogy, to swarm. And then Acts 10:38, calls attention to the fact that there are spirits of infirmities. This information draws my attention to the many diseases that are only detected by microscopes. Seeing microscopic cells that cause destruction. Keep in mind that every natural truth has a parallel spiritual truth. If something is not for Christ, it is against Him. So each one of those microscopic cells are influenced by a demon. In the realm of the spirit I have seen all sorts, sizes and shapes of demon spirits. This should give us confidence over diseases as much as we have confidence in our authority over a maggot. Bear in mind that satan is lord over the flies and flies are only mature maggots.

So maybe we are a Christian. Maybe I am a preacher and doing more good than bad. Maybe 90 percent of my life is totally yielded to God; that means 10 percent is yielded to satan. Well, who wants even 10 percent of torment? I want to destroy and stop all of the torment I can from my life and the lives of the people I love. Yes,

I am very narrow-minded. I know God is only good and refuse to believe anything else, since no sound Scripture supports anything but this truth. Yes, we can stay happy all the time!

The more we are influenced by the Holy Spirit the more effective we can be in ministry for God and the more God is able to use us. If I am yielded 90 percent, then there is 10 percent of me God cannot use. Before I can be a blessing, I have to be blessed. The more I have, the more I can give away. Jesus said to love your neighbor as yourself. If I have excess, I am not concerned about giving it away, because I will still have plenty for me and mine. If I have an excess of joy everywhere I go, I can give some away. And this world could sure use more joy. However, I'll be very stingy if I do not have excess.

Demonic influence is obvious when you knock on someone's door, as I have, and in the midst of our conversation, this person's voice, nature, attitude and physical appearance changes. And he says, "We have always been against you and your kind. Yeah, we've been around since they made the first wheel. I was there when they took that big old stone and began to knock the edges off it to make it round. We have always been around." And then he goes on to say, "You're so foolish to believe as you do. You have been deceived. After all, Mary was just a whore, just a prostitute. I was there; I know." Then he proceeded to curse Mary and then Jesus. It was very obvious that a demon was talking out of him.

However, by the same token, there are demons very much in operation who are just as destructive, but not so obvious. A spirit of paranoia is just as real as someone being used by a spirit of murder. Demons are demons. Their ultimate goal is torment – to take us to an eternal place of torment.

I want to use myself again as an illustration, because if I use someone else, it might not go over too well. All my life I have been a very sensitive person. I want you to notice in this illustration how demons observe us in order to become very FAMILIAR with us. I noticed in my school days and early years, people standing around and talking. Perhaps I would see one of them look over at me for a moment and then maybe the group would begin to laugh or something of that nature. It was at such a time that a spirit of paranoia saw an opportunity to use me, and thoughts began to run through my mind such as, "They are talking about you." I found such thoughts would come to my mind for the next few days such as, "Remember what your friend said the other day." This spirit would cause my mind to misconstrue or twist normal thought patterns. Usually I would find out later that something positive about me had been said.

So a spirit of paranoia had moved into my life and brought with him, not long after, a spirit of deception which is akin to a spirit of paranoia. Certain spirits work together. Some are very obvious even in the natural world. When you see someone who is naturally dirty, you will notice they were first lazy. Such people will also cheat since this is the lazy way to advance. Next a spirit of stealing will come. And finally, they will murder so they can steal, because they saw there was more to gain through stealing than through cheating. And it all started with laziness.

We need to understand this so we can stop these spirits before they get started. A spirit of paranoia will let in a spirit of deceit. As paranoia is deceit on a lower order, it promotes untruths. In Matthew 24, Jesus said, (and I paraphrase), "The first spirit and the leading spirit of the last days would be a spirit of deception."

But I have learned to make use of the characteristics

God originally gave me, instead of trying to be somebody I am not. I tried for years to hide my sensitive nature. This only caused more bondage, because it involved hypocrisy. So I have learned to let God use my characteristics instead of satan. I am still very sensitive, but I have become sensitive to other's hurts, feelings, sorrow and pain. This causes me to be sensitive to God and His paramount concern is people and their needs.

Take what you feel is a weakness and let God turn it into a treasure. Instead of allowing an evil spirit to express itself through you, allow the Holy Spirit.

We need to understand that demons will try to use our character. For instance, a person who is naturally meek and quiet is not normally used by a demon of boldness, not immediately anyway. Such a demon comes in the easier, not-so-obvious ways. There is a demonic boldness and a godly boldness. As I said earlier, all truth is parallel. For everything God has, satan has a counterfeit. By study of the Scriptures, you can learn to tell the difference between the real and the counterfeit. In fact, some situations can only be rightly divided by Scriptures; though many can be discerned by natural observation. Such is the case with boldness.

When demonic boldness is in operation, you can see evil demonstrated in a person's face, words, actions, etc. No peace, gentleness or kindness is displayed. But when godly boldness is in operation, such a person can become willing to lay down their life and open not their mouth. There is a calmness about such a person, along with a bravery so bold that all of hell trembles, and so gentle that hope is felt in their presence. In the midst of the worst storm, there is a kindness and gentleness that gives strength, comfort and draws attention to God. Yes, satan can use our characteristics, if we allow him to; but instead, we should let the Holy Spirit have free reign in our lives.

The Subtlety of Satan –

"But I fear, lest by any means, as the serpent beguiled Eve through his subtilty, so your minds should be corrupted from the simplicity that is in Christ," (2 Corinthians 11:3).

The Bible talks here about Adam and Eve being deceived by the subtlety of satan. Subtlety means trickery. You can see in this passage that trickery is also another demon spirit, because satan used trickery to beguile Eve. Today Christians still allow this spirit to use them; and I believe most of the reason is they do not realize it is an evil spirit. Sometimes Christians will trick people into a better deal maybe in a financial endeavor or try to get someone to do what they want for personal gain. This is trickery, and it is a demon that we need to cast out of our lives. We might say, "Well, this is just a little thing," but it obviously kept Adam and Eve from God's best for them. I am only trying to give you a few examples so you can LEARN to be more perceptive in dealing with the worst enemy of your person.

In Acts 5:3, the Bible says, concerning Ananias and Sapphira, "Why has satan filled thine heart to lie to the Holy Ghost?" What would cause this couple to do something so foolish that it cost them their lives? Many people will say, "I would never lie to God!" And you will not, until you have become accustomed to lying. If we are not FULLY truthful in filling out our taxes, then we are being used by a lying spirit. If it is not the truth, it is a lie. We might say it really isn't a whole lie; but Jesus said you are either for me or against me.

This spirit can grow within a person to the point that they will lie against God. Ananias and Sapphira lost their lives because they came before a congregation and stated, "Yes, we did just exactly what everyone else is doing. Yes, we did!" So boldly they lied! And they were not lying to

Peter and the church either. They lied to the Holy Ghost.

Yielding to a little lie is the first step toward lying to God, as well as the first step to eternal torment. Looking closer at Acts 5:3, we see that satan had filled their hearts to lie. So lying is of satan, all of it. Again, you can see the nature of lying is to benefit carnality, and carnality is an enemy against God. Everybody in that church made a covenant and said, "Let's all give a certain amount. Ananias and Sapphira agreed to do this. But they hid their profit where nobody could find it, and told everyone that they had done as everyone else in their giving. I want you to also notice that this wasn't a requirement from God or the church. They did not have to give anything. They chose to make that agreement. They could have been speaking out of the emotions of the moment or something of that nature. But in the end, they yielded to that spirit to which they were accustomed, but this time, its wages were death. It grew to that point.

Your Speech Must Be Sanctified –

"Let no corrupt communication proceed out of your mouth, but that which is good to the use of edifying, that it may minister grace unto the hearers," (Ephesians 4:29).

If the words of my mouth do not minister grace to the hearers and edify my hearers (edify means to build them up and strengthen them) then an evil spirit is using me.

It is either sin or holiness, nothing in between. The book of James says that if we will bridle our tongues, the Holy Spirit can use us. In fact, James says we can become perfect if we will just bridle our tongues. A perfect human being. Perfection then starts in the mouth. Yes, we can prevent demon forces from using us if we will control our mouths – making sure our mouths are used by the Holy Spirit and not an evil spirit.

So if the words of my mouth do not minister strength

to the people I am around (spiritual strength) and if they do not minister grace (unmerited favor) then the words of my mouth are corrupt words or satanic words. There really is no in-between; our words are either satanically-inspired or Holy Ghost-inspired.

"If any man speak, let him speak as the oracles of God; if any man minister, let him do it as of the ability which God giveth: that God in all things may be glorified through Jesus Christ, to whom be praise and dominion for ever and ever. Amen," (1 Peter 4:11).

If you speak, speak only the oracles of God. Do not speak unless your words glorify God, give grace to the hearers, draw your hearers to God and comfort them with God's goodness. Every conversation we have should be a three-party conversation. As we are listening to someone, before making any kind of a reply, we should ask the Holy Spirit exactly what we should say. Do not let a spirit of intimidation try to influence you into thinking you are inferior just because God does not give you anything to say. Just be bold and say, "I do not know at this time what the Holy Spirit would have me say. But if you so desire, as I wait upon Him concerning this issue, I will let you know as soon as I get a perception from him."

I cannot put enough emphasis on our not allowing the kingdom of darkness to use us in our speech. Proverbs 18:21, says death and life are in the power of the tongue. 1 Peter 1:15-16, says, *"But as he which hath called you is holy, so be ye holy in all manner of conversation;*

"Because it is written, Be ye holy; for I am holy," (1 Peter 1:15, 16).

This Scripture then goes on to give us instructions on how to be holy in ALL manner of conversation. If we want more of God's holiness and His reputation to be seen and known in this world, we are going to have to start at first base which is – BE HOLY, BEGINNING WITH THE WORDS OF OUR MOUTHS.

I pray you do not take some of this strong teaching as a promotion of bondage, condemnation or guilt, for such thinking could not be further from the main thrust of my life and this book. My intention is to give hungry hearts a truth that they have been longing for. Please allow the Holy Spirit to give you the grace of this teaching. Think of this, not as a promotion of condemnation, but rather direction whereby the exceedingly great and precious holy treasures of God can be manifested in your flesh.

"For God, who commanded the light to shine out of darkness, hath shined in our hearts, to give the light of the knowledge of the glory of God in the face of Jesus Christ.

"But we have this treasure in earthen vessels, that the excellency of the power may be of God, and not of us.

"We are toubled on every side, yet not distressed; we are perplexed, but not in despair;

"Persecuted, but not forsaken; cast down, but not destroyed;

"Always bearing about in the body the dying of the Lord Jesus, that the life also of Jesus might be made manifest in our body," (2 Corinthians 4:6-10).

Think of it as a privilege offered to the world, but you are one of the few who has found it. Such a divine treasure hidden from the foundation of the world and now you have found a way for it to be manifested in you. And that treasure is THE HOPE OF THE AGES, THE MYSTERY OF THE AGES, which is CHRIST IN YOU THE HOPE OF GOD BEING GLORIFIED.

"Even the mystery which hath been hid from ages and from generations, but now is made manifest to his saints:

"To whom God would make known what is the riches of the glory of this mystery among the Gentiles; which is Christ in you, the hope of glory:" (Colossians 1:26,27).

There was a time in which God had so much confidence that Christ would glorify Him, that He sent Him to this earth. And Christ did just that – He glorified the Father well. And Jesus paid the price so that now the church can glorify God as Jesus did and in even greater measure. (See John 14:12-14.) Also you will see this same truth in Ephesians 1:17-23. It is an opportunity to wear God's honor, holiness, pureness, dignity and His reputation.

"Herein is our love made perfect, that we may have boldness in the day of judgment: because as he is, so are we in this world," (1 John 4:17).

God is a God of grace, and to be Christ-like is to be the same. We need to talk like He talks. Sometimes we do not want to give someone words that are kind, merciful and graceful. As our sensibilities say, "They do not deserve such words. Only a godly person should have such words spoken to them. Do you know what they said to me last week? Do you know what they did? I'm not going to tell them that I love them or I'm proud of them, or how great I think they are! It's not true. They are not great! They need to feel guilty for what they have done or said in the past!"

To give people words that they do not deserve is grace. It's speaking like God speaks. It's acting like God acts. That's the reason we are saved.

"But love ye your enemies, and do good, and lend, hoping for nothing again; and your reward shall be great, and ye shall be the children of the Highest: for he is kind unto the unthankful and to the evil.

"Be ye therefore merciful, as your Father also is merciful," (Luke 6:35,36).

Trickery and deception are the opposite of the wisdom of God. For example, trickery and deception are in operation to get people to do something for selfish reasons. The opposite of such is the wisdom of God – getting people to do something so they can have more of the abundant life God has already provided for them. I win more people to the Lord this way than any other way. I treat them and talk to them like they are something very valuable and precious, like they are the holiness of God. Remember death and life are in the words of our mouths. We need to make sure our words are giving people life.

I also use this wisdom of God to mature the saints of God. Talk to them like you have confidence and trust in them, as though they had the mind of Christ. Let us pull out the good in people's lives. Let's magnify the good. Everybody has some good, so let's look for it and magnify it. It's hard for me to believe that there are people who do not have at least 20 percent good in them.

It has been easy for the Body of Christ to find the bad in our eternal brothers and sisters. And the truth is they probably had a much higher percentage of good than bad. But many have been destroyed because the good has never been mentioned while the bad has been amplified.

Let's magnify the good and win our loved ones to the Lord and then we'll have the anointing to win our neighbors and our world. I've won alcoholics and drug addicts to the Lord by telling them how the goodness of God is seen in their lives. I would look at and magnify the good. The goodness of God is seen in the lives of the worst, if we'll just look for it. Yes, God can use a drug addict. God is greater in power and ability than satan. So let us magnify what God is doing in lives and we'll see a change as the amplified good starts growing bigger. There is power when we use God's power and His power is His Words. (See Romans 1:16.)

So let His Words abide in our mouths, so we can change our loved one's eternal destiny. Very soon we will walk on streets of gold. It will be worth all of the dying out to what flesh wants to do, when we walk on those streets with our loved ones, knowing they are there because they heard God's graceful, merciful words from our lips. Isn't our Heavenly Father so good!

CHAPTER 7

Understanding Warfare

I'm convinced that many people's prayers are not answered because they are not knowledgeable of the fact that there is a demonic spiritual world. The demonic world's greatest purpose is to withhold blessings of God from humanity. We need to arrive at the knowledge that there are demon forces assigned especially to the Christian for the purpose of keeping God's goodness from him. If we can mature with this knowledge, more and more of our prayers will be manifested in this natural world.

First of all, we must understand we are in warfare. 2 Corinthians 10:3,4, mentions the weapons of our warfare. So it is clear that in the days of Apostle Paul, there was spiritual warfare. We must understand so much more today, because the devil is coming down to us with GREAT WRATH, because HE KNOWS he has but a short time. (See Revelation 12:12, Matthew 24:4-20,21,22, Isaiah 14:16, and 2 Timothy 3:1 for Scripture supporting these thoughts.)

"Fight the good fight of faith, lay hold on eternal life, whereunto thou art also called, and hast professed a good profession before many witnesses," (1 Timothy 6:12).

FIGHT the good fight of faith. Fighting denotes strenuous efforts being put forth. Philippians 2:9, teaches us that we have a Name that is above every name. That Name is Jesus. EVERY knee must bow and give reverence to, surrender to, yield its strength to the Name of Jesus. Any name you can think of, such as cancer, lack, poverty, arthritis, etc., must surrender to that more powerful Name.

Yes, we are in warfare; but our adversary is limited in weaponry and power, and we are not. We must discern these evil spirits and cast them out of our lives. In Ephesians 6:11, we are told to put on the whole armor of God, that we may be able to withstand the wiles of the devil. Again, it is clear that there is a warfare going on. And the only way we can withstand and be victorious is to put on the whole ARMOR OF GOD. Why?

"For we wrestle not against flesh and blood, but against principalities, against powers, against the rulers of the darkness of this world, against spiritual wickedness in high places," Ephesians 6:12).

Another word that is co-equal with "wrestle" is "violence." Scripture plainly reveals the strenuous, violent, spiritual warfare raging against us. For years I have been unfaithful in teaching vital, Scriptural truths that the Lord has given me. Primarily I haven't because every time I would start teaching some of these truths, I and my family were plagued with unprecedented, uncalled-for, nonsensical opposition in every area of our lives, as well as opposition from people because of the teaching.

We Americans think we are too intelligent to lower ourselves to believe in the realm of the spiritual, especially the evil-spirit world. Very few preachers teach on this subject. Those who do look peculiar and are often ridiculed. That is hard on the flesh and pride. But pride is selfish, and we all need to die out to self so the Lord can work through us more proficiently. So my deliberation is to please the Lord, and I pray it blesses all. And to those it does not bless, I am sorry; but to the best of my ability, I must obey the Holy Spirit. Time is too short for church games. Besides, whether we want to acknowledge it or not, the battle is raging. I am so grieved in my spirit as many of our front-line combat troops are dying right and left because of a lack of knowledge about their worst enemy.

"Lest Satan should get an advantage of us: for we are not ignorant of his devices," (2 Corinthians 2:11).

Again, let us die to self so Jesus can live in us. Then if people are critical toward us, their criticism is really directed toward Jesus and not at us.

This chapter is designed to equip the saint with weapons that are not carnal but rather are spiritual and mighty. Once again, we can destroy the works of the enemy that has been assigned to destroy God's goodness in the lives of humanity. I believe this chapter is assigned to the ELITE of the green beret in God's army. The green beret is the elite of all armies. But the elite of the green beret would be the elite of the elite and would have the greatest overcoming skills. If you are the least in the army of God, this message will help make you the elite of God's green beret, if you adhere to the message and heartbeat of God.

"Because the foolishness of God is wiser than men; and the weakness of God is stronger than men.

"For ye see your calling, brethren, how that not many wise men after the flesh, not many mighty, not many noble, are called:

"But God hath chosen the foolish things of the world to confound the wise; and God hath chosen the weak things of the world to confound the things which are mighty;" (1 Corinthians 1:25-27).

Who Is On The Lord's Side? –

This is a mature message. I want to deal now with some simple but profound facts that will help bring about maturity. One of the facts you need to understand in warfare is: you cannot be on both sides of the battle. It is life-threatening to even try to be on the enemy's side and on the home-army side at the same time. James 1:7,8, says that a double-minded person will receive nothing from the Lord.

I know this is a primary area of failure for God's people. Everything we say or think on at length should be ordained of God.

"Let the words of my mouth, and the meditations of my heart, be acceptable in thy sight, O lord, my strength, and my redeemer," (Psalms 19:14).

We are on one side or the other. Let me clarify the subject of our thought life. We cannot stop "a" thought from satan being presented to us, but we can control what we do with that thought. Do we cast it out? Or do we let it lead us to the next step which is imagination followed by sin?

Thoughts not given to imagination, word or deed are unborn sin. Jesus said something that I want to bring out that gives more authentication to our train of thought of being on one side or the other. His statement is going to hurt, but it is going to hurt real "good."

I can remember working at a lumber yard back in 1970, and I got a very large splinter in my hand. I dug and dug into my hand with a pocket knife until I was able to get the splinter out. As the splinter was on its way out, it hurt real "good."

Well, Jesus said in Luke 11:23, that we are either for Him or against Him. We must understand this first step and when we do, we are on our way to becoming an ELITE, green beret, combat trooper in God's army. Keep in mind this elite group will get victory when nobody else can. Those who stay and guard the compound are not in this group. The elite are not interested in staying in the comfort zone. They are aggressive, constantly winning battles, always having victory, because they are always looking for and finding the enemy, even the most cunning and keenly-trained enemy. The elite of the elite always possess the land. Too many Christians are victorious only on Sunday morning.

If 3,000 people would get saved in 99.9 of our churches today, we would be doing a greater miracle than the Apostle Peter who got 3,000 saved in one service. The reason is people are not supposed to get saved at church. The church should be trained enough to be able to get the 3,000 saved in the streets and then bring them to church so they too can mature and do the work of the ministry of Christ.

"And he gave some, apostles; and some, prophets; and some, evangelists; and some, pastors and teachers;

"For the perfecting of the saints, for the work of the ministry, for the edifying of the body of Christ:

"Till we all come in the unity of the faith, and of the knowledge of the Son of God, unto a perfect man, unto the measure of the stature of the fulness of Christ:" (Ephesians 4:11-13).

This is the perfect will of God. For you see, you will not find 3,000 sinners in our Bible-believing churches in a particular service.

We are either for Christ or against Him; either influenced by an evil spirit or the Holy Spirit; and either hearers of the Words and Oracles of God or hearers of the unctions of satan.

"If any man speak, let him speak as the oracles of God; if any man minister, let him do it as of the ability which God giveth: that God in all things may be glorified through Jesus Christ, to whom be praise and dominion

for ever and ever. Amen," (1 Peter 4:11).

Also see Ephesians 4:29; 5:4-7; and Psalms 19:14 for further reference on this.

No Neutral Ground – Another area in which satan has greatly hindered the church is by perpetuating the lie that, "I am not being used in words, actions or deeds by satan, and yes, I know, neither am I being used of God. I am just in the flesh. I am in carnality, just on neutral ground." Colossians 1:13, plainly teaches there are only two eternal kingdoms. You can find much Scripture to support this truth. There is a kingdom of light and the kingdom of darkness. Romans 8:7, also supports this truth when it says, "Because the carnal mind is enmity against God: for it is not subject to the law of God, neither indeed can be."

So if we are in the flesh, we are influenced by satan, because carnality is an enemy against God. You cannot be on neutral ground in a war. You are influenced by one kingdom or the other. Someone might say, "Well, I am not on the enemy's side. I just use some of his words occasionally." *In war using the enemy's words will get you killed.*

Galatians 5:16, plainly teaches us to walk (putting natural and mental expression to God's Word) in the Spirit (His Word) and thus not fulfill the lust of the flesh. Notice we have no third choice. We are either walking in the Spirit or fulfilling the lust of the flesh. I know this hurts – but God today is calling His saints to maturity. He must have some keenly-trained, elite, green beret, combat troops who can find the enemy that has been in our compounds for years. And we have even accepted them into our ranks as friends. But these not-so-obvious spirits, so inconspicuous that most of the church world doesn't even consider them evil spirits, are undercover agents from satan who are hindering what God wants to do in His church.

God wants to do something supernatural, very extraordinary, something quite holy. He has said we must be holy in all manner of conversation. Holiness begins in our conversation. We must realize we are at war! One of the not-so-obvious evil spirits that has lamed the churches are those words that are not God ordained.

Keep Your Armor On –

Going on to another factor that the elite of the elite know and practice is ALWAYS keeping your armor on. 1 Peter 5:8, teaches that satan is seeking whom he may devour. Then notice the next verse, verse 9, where it says satan resists those who are stedfast in the faith.

During my school days, my family moved several times. Sometimes I would go to 2 or 3 schools in one year. And I always had the problem of having to prove myself in each new school. The tough guys always had to find out how you ranked. I noticed if you whipped them hard enough they didn't bother you anymore. I also noticed they may say something from a great distance. And if they saw you coming, they would run off.

That is the way the devil is. If you whip him with the Word of God, he will keep his distance from you, but he will always come back, because demonic persistance is part of his nature. He comes back primarily to see if you're sick in spirit from not feeding on God's Word. Just like the tough guys in school who were whipped real good, satan would like to get you in a position where he could give you double what you gave him. If you do not stay sober (watchful) in keeping the Word of God in your life, you will become weak and satan will find you.

We must keep our armor on; sleep with it on, because we are at war. The devil will say, "That sounds like bondage." However, God's goodness is not bondage. If it isn't good, rendering joy, fulfillment and satisfaction, then it is not of God. Religion (doctrines of men and devils) equals bondage. But God's abundant life equals tranquility. So the elite must never remove their armor. We must always be watchful (sober) of the enemy sneaking into our lives. More Christians backslide in time of vacation, because they also take a vacation from God. While on vacation they take their armor off and are not sober and watchful. That is just what the enemy is waiting for. Never remove joy, peace, happiness and life sublime, because nothing is better and to do so would mean putting on torment.

Be Vigilant –

1 Peter 5:8, also tells us to be vigilant. In the Greek there are some other words that are co-equal in meaning. They are: active and aggressive. If we are going to be the elite of the elite, we need to be actively and aggressively looking for the enemy or for sign of his presence. If we are only sober (watchful in guarding the territory immediately around us) we will be successful in that area only. For example, a person would be like a great champion of a soldier who could master anything the enemy throws at him; but he never leaves his back yard. This guy will have very little success.

If God says, "You can possess the world," but you never leave your back yard, you will have a nice back yard. But you will never enjoy the showers of blessings that you haven't room enough to receive. If we are going to be vigilant, we will have to be like a bloodhound, searching until we find the criminal. I am out looking for any signs of the works of darkness that may be trying to spoil my life, so I can put a stop to them. I am not just on the defense, I am also on the offense. I am not just going to wait until there is an obvious sign that the enemy is in my life; because by then, most of the time, it is too late. Instead, I am going to find the enemies before they find me, even the well-kept, hidden enemies in my private life.

A good boxer is one who doesn't just set back and wait for his opponent. Rather, he aggressively goes to him to overtake him. Jesus said it this way, "The gates of hell shall not prevail against us." Gates do not move; they are stationary. The elite of the elite will aggressively storm the gates of hell. We must look for EVERY CHANCE, every microscopic chance, to defeat the enemy's plans to spoil us.

Discernment of Demons –

Anyone born again has authority over the worst attack of the most fierce demon or even satan himself. But if the person is spirit-filled, they will be more sensitive and accurate in the realm of the spirit. God says He will not allow ANYTHING to happen until first He lets His children know about it. (See Amos 3:7 and Matthew 11:11.) If the spirit-filled believer has the gift of discerning of spirits operating in his life, he will become more supernaturally accurate and proficient in dealing with evil spirits. Now let's deal with a train of thought that I believe has been greatly overlooked – coming to the SIMPLE KNOWLEDGE OF DISCERNMENT OF EVIL SPIRITS.

The discerning of spirits is a gift that is given, the other is learned from the Scripture and through maturity in your walk with the Holy Spirit. When the gift of discerning of spirits is in operation, the five physical senses SEEM to be in operation but they are not. It is simply your spirit duplicating the five physical senses in the realm of the Spirit. At first when being used by this gift, you actually believe your five physical senses are relating to the realm of the experience, because the experience is so real. And it is real, because the spirit world is more real than the physical. Also the spiritual is eternal, and the best of the natural is very temporal.

So let us deal with the simple understanding of discernment of evil spirits. You will find that discernment of evil spirits is learned; it is like the gift of discerning of spirits, but it is not as pronounced, supernatural or spiritual as, for example, the gift of faith versus faith that comes from the knowledge of God's Word. If the body of Christ will walk with diligence in the light that has already been given them, God will move them on to greater maturity. I believe if the church will learn what the Bible has to say about discernment, God will move them on to the gift of discerning of spirits to cause them to be more accurate and proficient in dealing with the enemy.

Hebrews 5:14, says, *"But strong meat belongeth to them that are of full age, even those who by reason of use have their senses exercised to discern both good and evil."*

We are living in a day in which I am so shocked at supposedly-mature Christians who cannot discern good from evil. They honestly do not know. That tells me that they either do not know the will of God from not taking time to read it, or they do not continue in the Word. As 1 Corinthians 15:2, tells us, we are saved (or have all that God has provided for us in both the natural and the spiritual) if we keep the Word in our minds. Romans 10:17, says that faith comes by hearing, not having heard.

I have been guilty of thinking that I "have it," because I have already given ten years to that teaching. The Greek word also means giving audience to. So I need to hear, think, meditate and read about the riches of God's goodness to me continually. In Matthew 4:4, Jesus said that we cannot stay alive by natural bread alone. If we are going to stay alive spiritually, we must continually feed upon the bread of life. A Christian who is dead cannot tell the difference from good or evil, even though they once could. A Christian who is suffering from malnutrition is so weak he cannot tell the difference from good and evil, even though he once could.

The real problem is that Christians suffer BURNOUT.

There is one simple reason why: they have gotten into "religion." Religion is doctrines of man and devils, and it is sin. Sin has its wages which are death. If you find "life," you will never die. For example, let's say you recently discovered that you had an uncle who just died. He owned one-fourth of the world's wealth and had made you his sole heir. Now the will is sent to you. Anybody in their right mind would have the will memorized within a very short period of time, even if they had claimed not to have the gift of memorization in the past. In this case, I am sure they could also tell you exactly where the things are that they love the most, like exactly where the goodies are that are making them overweight. Even an animal memorizes the things it loves most.

I am not condemning at all; I am making the point that Christians do not know the truth about the real nature of God. If they only knew that His highest priority, the paramount issue of His supreme, divine person is that YOU WOULD HAVE GOD'S BEST OUT OF EVERY AREA OF THIS LIFE. (See 2 Peter 1:2-4 and 3 John 2.)

God has left a will that all the earth in its most powerful setting with its most powerful courts, as well as the most powerful demonic forces of hell, cannot stop from being expedited! If people only knew the riches of His goodness, the depth of His purpose to have manifested a life for them beyond their fondest dreams or imaginations. And it is all in His will. All we have to do is read it and act like it is true, just as you would any other will.

"FOR THUS SAITH THE HOLY SPIRIT, EYE HATH NOT SEEN, NEVER HAS THERE BEEN AN EAR TO HEAR, NOR EVER HAS IT ENTERED THE MIND OR SPIRIT THE RICHES OF MY GOODNESS, YES, THE DEEP THINGS OF GOD THAT I HAVE PREPARED FOR YOU. BUT I WILL REVEAL THEM TO YOU BY MY WORD WHEN IT BECOMES

SPIRIT, MY HIGHEST EXPRESSION OF MY PER-SON TO YOU."

So if we discover what the Scriptures will do for us, we will automatically get into it and be supernaturally accurate in discerning good from evil. The word "discern" also means to "judge, determine, perceive or to see to obtain knowledge by the senses." So in understanding the five physical senses, I can relate them to the Word of God and discern what is of satan or what is of God. If my eyes say it's of God or of the devil, then I can know. If we do not KNOW if something is of God, then cast it away from you, without hesitation, because it could be a matter of life or death for you! Remember we are at war!

Methods of Discernment –

On the battlefield if you find something that you are not sure whether it is intended to bless you or blow you away, always THINK LIFE. Yes, we can discern with our five physical senses if an evil spirit is involved. Does what you smell, taste, look, touch, hear or see glorify God? If not, cast it out the same way you would get rid of a bomb that is designed to destroy you and your loved ones. By following this simple teaching, you will be able to discern evil spirits in their simplest forms. This simple teaching, if hearkened to, will also cause you to be on your way to becoming an elite of the elite – winning, surviving and being blessed when no one else is.

Another method of discernment is talking to people and listening to what they say. Do their words honor and glorify God? If not, we have discerned an evil spirit. If they are always talking sickness, it is simply a spirit of infirmity. (See Acts 10:38.) Someone who is always physically abusing others has a spirit of violence.

We can learn, in the simple form, how to cast out evil spirits. We will deal with this subject in greater detail later on. But let me just say at this time, God is the opposite of satan. So you can just do the opposite of what the evil spirit is doing. For example, light drives out darkness. Love does the same to hate. Simply judge with your five physical senses.

The Gift of Discerning of Spirits –

"to another discerning of spirits;... (1 Corinthians 12:10).

As I said earlier, spiritual discernment is like the natural gift or learned discernment, except the spiritual gift is more supernatural, more spiritual, more accurate and more pronounced. Until one matures in this gift, he really believes he is seeing, hearing, smelling, tasting and feeling in the natural, when it is really the spirit duplicating the five physical senses. We need all of this understanding so we can learn to deal with hindering evil spirits and stop them. Keep in mind, if there is a problem, deal with the source of the problem. If you don't, the problem will not only persist, it will get worse. Learn not to focus your greatest attention on people or the natural arena in which the problem is being manifested. Spirits are being discerned, not people.

Years ago I had been dealing with a person whose behavior was quite obviously out of the will of God, so much so that even a semi-carnal Christian could see they were in sin. In fact, this person knew and admitted to the sin. I had dealt with them for years, teaching the Word or trying to anyway. Things did get better, and really this person would like to have stopped their sin involvement but just couldn't stay victorious for long.

This was back in 1978, and we lived at 139 Tulip Tree in Harvester, MO. I was awakened during the night session as I perceived someone's presence in the bedroom. As I awakened, I quickly got out of bed, because there were two man-like creatures, ugly and vicious looking, standing by my bedside. I got out of bed, swinging my fists, only to hear and see these creatures laughing. Since they were demonic spirits, I could do nothing to them physically. My attempts at attacking them were only a joke. In the realm of the spirit volumes of information can be obtained momentarily. And the Lord spoke to me in my spirit and said, "The person you have been dealing with – this is their problem. Each one of these spirits represent a major problem in their life."

I rebuked the spirits from my presence and for the next few months, when that person would come to my mind, I would rebuke those spirits. The next time I saw him, he even looked different in the natural. There was a peace about him that registered on his face. He was absolutely free from those problems.

All truth is parallel. You can mow your yard, year after year, and it will not look too bad. But if you want to really get rid of the weeds, you have to get to the ROOT OF THE PROBLEM!

Stopping the Enemy –

In earlier sections, we saw how to find the enemy. So now let us look at how to stop him. We have pretty much dealt with this train of thought already, but we need to look more closely at the power we have in the Name of Jesus. God has given us a Name that is above every name, and that Name is Jesus, the Word of God.

"And the Word was made flesh, and dwelt among us, (and we beheld his glory, the glory as of the only begotten of the Father,) full of grace and truth," (John 1:14).

Every problem has a name, and it MUST surrender to the Word of God.

"Wherefore God also hath highly exalted him, and given him a name which is above every name," (Philippians

2:9).

We must use unrelenting determination in following the will of God for our lives. I am reminded of a story I heard about a family driving down the highway. As they drove, the father needed to look out the rear view mirror and noticed his son was standing up blocking his view. So he asked him very politely, "Son, would you please sit down? You are blocking my view from the rear view mirror."

They had driven on down the road for some distance when the father noticed his son still standing. He asked him again, with a little bit more authority to sit down. This went on until the father threatened to give him a whipping if he didn't sit down. The father drove on and looked in the rear view moirror only to see his son still standing. So he stopped the car and whipped the boy. As the family drove on down the highway, after a few minutes they heard the little boy whisper, "I may be sitting down on the outside, but on the inside, I am still standing up!"

This is exactly how we need to deal with the problems of life – let them know you are standing up on the inside. Mr. devil, I do not care what the natural appearance may say, I have the Word of God inside me and on the inside, I have final authority and will continue to stand on it, no matter what. Remember Ephesians 6:13,14 – after you have done all to stand, then keep on standing on God's Word, because it will never return void (Isaiah 55:11).

Casting Out Evil Spirits With a Clean Mind –

"When the unclean spirit is gone out of a man, he walketh through dry places, seeking rest, and findeth none.

"Then he saith, I will return into my house from whence I came out; and when he is come, he findeth it

empty, swept and garnished.

"Then goeth he, and taketh with himself seven other spirits more wicked than himself, and they enter in and dwell there: and the last state of the man is worse than the first. Even so shall it be also unto this wicked generation," (Matthew 12:43-45).

The Bible says when an unclean spirit is gone out of an individual, the spirit will come back with others that are worse than he. I'm reminded of the time my wife and I pastored a church in Taylor, Texas. In the parsonage at 707 Lizzie Street, in the east bedroom, our bed sat against the south wall. During the night session, I had the worst experience with demons I had ever had up to that time. I was awakened by a strong perception that evil spirits were in the room. This was the very first time I did not see them, but only heard them in the spirit. I will have to say that up to this time, I had never had a more horrifying, tormenting experience. There were about six evil spirits in the room, and they were making all sorts of tormenting sounds, horrible moans and groans which could not be duplicated in this natural world, because their noise was demonically supernatural.

I have often said that this is the reason so many people who are abusing drugs lose their minds. When you cancel out the natural, the spiritual is very real. And if it were demonic influences that promoted you to cancel out the natural, your confrontation with an evil, demonic kingdom (a demonic world in which natural man cannot survive) could result in a person literally being scared to death.

Anyway, I rebuked those evil spirits, as Jesus told me to. But this time nothing happened. I was more violent in my determination to rebuke them, but still nothing happened. In fact, I believe they grew worse with their hideous noises. In my spirit, I cried out to the Lord with my whole heart and said, "Lord, you told me if I would rebuke the evil spirits, they would leave. Lord, You have to help me because their torment will destroy me within moments if they are not stopped!"

Jesus spoke to me, and I learned volumes of information that night. He said, "There are different ways to rebuke different types of demons. This kind can only be rebuked by filling your mind with my Word, so that your thought patterns are directly in line with my Word."

"Thou wilt keep him in perfect peace, whose mind is stayed on thee: because he trusteth in thee," (Isaiah 26:3).

I knew I would die within moments if the torment didn't stop, so immediately I began to think on any Scripture I had PREVIOUSLY memorized. (Folks, please do not try to build your house when in the storm. I have never known anyone who has.) I noticed immediately that the torment began to leave. But the moment I stopped to see if the demons and their torment were gone, they returned with at least the same amount of torment. So immediately I forced my mind back into the Word of God and again they left. But just as before, when I stopped to check on their condition, they were back just as strong as ever, maybe even a little worse. I did this, I believe, three times. I have been a slow learner in the past, but once I got it, it was rock solid. I never checked again,and I DO NOT KNOW when they left.

Jesus said in John 15:3, that we are made clean and pure by His Words. We can stay clean from the torment of the devil if we will keep our minds stayed on His Word. But so many Christians are continually tormented, BECAUSE THEY KEEP USING THEIR SENSES TO CHECK AND SEE IF THE TORMENT IS GONE – TO SEE IF GOD'S WORD IS TRUTH. You could say it this way and be extremely accurate in accordance with God's Word: IF YOU WILL CHECK WITH YOUR PHYSICAL SENSES TO SEE IF GOD'S WORD IS TRUE, YOU WILL BE TORMENTED TO DEATH!

So Matthew 12:43-45, is very much an actual reality to me. Evil spirits will leave, because the Word will absolutely cast them out. But they will come back to see if there is any room for them. However, if we are full of light, there is no room for darkness. In fact, light torments the darkness.

CHAPTER 8

How People Become Demon Possessed

In this chapter I want to show the progressive steps even a Christian can take to become demon possessed. I want to make it clear that once a Christian finally gives totally into satan and becomes demon possessed, they are no longer a Christian. There are progressive steps that a Christian must take, however, before they could become possessed by the devil.

Degrees of Possession –

There are three degrees or stages of being demon possessed or vexed by evil spirits. As you explore this train of thought, you will find in the King James Bible the words "possess" and "vexed" are co-equal in meaning, especially in the Scriptures I will use in this chapter.

You will also notice from this chapter that with each level of possession or vexation, there are different degrees. Notice for instance, in 1 Peter 2:21 and 4:1, where we read about Jesus suffering for us. The Greek word "suffer" or "suffered" is co-equal in meaning with "vexed." Throughout the Scriptures we see people who clearly were demon possessed and vexed with an evil spirit.

"Lord, have mercy on my son: for he is lunatick, and sore vexed: for ofttimes he falleth into the fire, and oft into the water," (Matthew 17:15).

Here the word "vexed" carries exactly the same meaning in the Greek as the word "suffer" does in 1 Peter 2:21; 4:1. Anybody who has remotely read the Bible knows Jesus was not demon vexed as was the man of Matthew. Jesus was simply demon harrassed, tempted, oppressed; or, you could say, satan offered Him opportunities to sin. (See Matthew 4.) Yet, Jesus never accepted, for He was without sin.

The point is, the simple knowledge of both of these passages show us that, Number One, both were the exact same Greek word except one was translated as vexed and the other as suffer; and Number Two, it is clearly known that both refer to entirely different experiences of satanic harassment.

Without going any further in this study one can plainly understand that there are different degrees or stages of satanic vexation.

Steps to Possession –

So now let's look at three distinct, progressive steps leading to a demon-possessed spirit, mind and body. As you study the Bible you will find the first step towards being demon possessed in spirit, soul and body is being tempted or oppressed by satan. You will find by comparing Scripture with Scripture that "tempted" or "oppressed" are co-equal terms. Let me give some clarity on an issue before we go on. Religion (doctrines of man) has said that one who is demon possessed is taken over by that evil spirit – soul and body. However, Scriptures reveal some cases in which a person is possessed by an evil spirit, and plainly does not have the same torment as another. One is tormented in their spirit, mind and body, while the other is only tormented by a thought.

If a thought is from satan, then, of course, satan possesses that thought; and that thought when injected in the human mind instantly causes torment. So as long as a person has a possessed thought from satan, they have a degree of satan possessing their life. I want to do my best to make this clear for two main reasons. Number One, I have more confidence, respect, love, admiration and honor for the Lord Jesus Christ than anything or anyone, even my own life. And I know the Scriptures are true when they say, "He was tempted." YET HE WAS WITHOUT SIN. Number Two, I want people to understand that they are not bad people just because a thought comes into their mind that is not of God. At the same time I want poeple to know the DANGER involved in receiving a thought that is not of God, because this can be the first step in being possessed, spirit, soul and body, particularly if they give EXTENDED THOUGHT to it or add word or deed to it.

You will notice in Hebrews 4:15, that Jesus was in all points tempted as we, but did not sin. In addition, Matthew 4, is plain in its speech concerning Jesus being tempted (given the opportunity to become demon possessed). But we need to understand temptation is not sin; it is what you do with that temptation. You will notice in your Bible studies that satan has always used these progressional steps in order to possess a life. In Genesis 3, Eve fell and lost out to satan because she yielded to (accepted and acted upon) the thought sent by satan. This thought was against God; it was a vexation in her mind. It is so important for us to know the Word of God; because satan will take the Word of God and pull it out of context just enough to pervert it and provoke us to sin. Just as he told Adam and Eve, "If you partake of this, you will be just like God," (satan's promotion was you will BE GOD) so today he tempts with the same temptations.

"For though we walk in the flesh, we do not war after the flesh:

"(For the weapons of our warfare are not carnal, but mighty through God to the pulling down of strong holds;)

"Casting down imaginations, and every high thing that exalteth itself against the knowledge of God, and bringing into captivity every thought to the obedience of Christ;" (2 Corinthians 10:3-5).

Here we see the three progressional steps that one must take in order to become demon possessed in spirit, mind and body. It clearly teaches that the thought realm, which is oppression, is the first step toward full possession. Secondly, it teaches that the imagination realm, which is an obsession stage, is the second stage. Imagination is simply purposely entertaining a thought for an extended period of time. Last it teaches about the third step which is the stronghold stage and the final step. At this point a person becomes possessed of an evil spirit in his mind (soul) body and spirit.

Now let us examine each step, starting with the first step, which is oppression, vexation and temptation. The first step is simple to accept or reject and is the thought realm.

"And delivered just Lot, vexed with the filthy conversation of the wicked:

"(For that righteous man dwelling among them, in seeing and hearing, vexed his righteous soul from day to day with their unlawful deeds);" (2 Peter 2:7,8).

Here the Scriptures say Lot was vexed in his righteous soul day by day by their FILTHY CONVERSATION and their unlawful deeds. We need to make sure that our close associations are with people to whom we are equally yoked, those who are at least born-again Christians. If we do not, we will NOT win them over. Instead, they will win us over because we have dishonored the holy direction for our lives – the Holy Word of God. In 2 John 10,11, we are told that, "If there come any unto you and bring not this doctrine, receive him not into your house...." or have no close association. If you do, you are a partaker of their sin, the same sin they are in.

Be Not Unequally Yoked –

Those who are considering marriage to an unbeliever should beware! You are out of the will of God and there is a 90 percent chance you will end up with a wrecked life because of divorce.

We must be Scripturally smart. Satan will use a half truth to get us to submit to his first step of torment, yes, the first step to becoming fully demon possessed. He will say, "Well, who do you think you are? After all, Jesus Himself ate with sinners!" That is a half-truth, because Jesus wasn't there for socializing. He was there on business, not to fulfill fleshly pleasure. He was on a heavenly assignment. In addition, Jesus didn't have a continued relationship of any kind with these people, unless they yielded to the goodness of God and became a follower of Christ.

The Bible teaches us plainly that we are the light of the world, and we should not have fellowhsip with darkness. I am not saying that we shouldn't be full of God's goodness, kindness and caring. We should display these godly characteristics and hunger for the opportunity to be involved with people who are hungry for the truth in their lives. Yes, we should have them over for a nice meal and accept their invitations, as Jesus did. But do not put on a religious front, and do not compromise. If you compromise to win someone to the Lord, you lose! Always know the goodness of God is not offensive. You will not offend anyone for representing God, no matter what they say.

We need to understand the importance of not yielding to satan's first attempts to gain control of our lives. If satan cannot get you to give in to the first step, he will never get you into the second. And the third hasn't a shade of a chance. Lot was vexed in his mind as the filthy conversation and evil deeds provoked him to thought. Everyone is tempted and vexed if they draw themselves into a position in which sin is knowingly present.

"But every man is tempted, when he is drawn away of his own lust, and enticed," (James 1:14).

If you know satan is in something, don't put yourself in that position. It is bad enough for sin to be brought to you, but it is crazy to knowingly expose yourself to sin.

Our Minds Need Renewal –

We need to have our minds so reprogrammed by the Word that when any conversation or any thought is offered to us, our minds will work like a computer, analyzing each situation with the questions: "Is this in line with the Word? Does this give glory to God?" If not, or if in doubt, cast it out. If our minds are not transformed or at least in an active process of being transformed to the things of God (His Word) then we are open season for satan to take us through the progressional steps.

"I beseech you therefore, brethren, by the mercies of God, that ye present your bodies a living sacrifice, holy, acceptable unto God, which is your reasonable service.

"And be not conformed to this world: but be ye transformed by the renewing of your mind, that ye may prove what is that good, and acceptable, and perfect, will of God," (Romans 12:1,2).

Many Christians get into trouble in this area. Though they have been born again for years, they have never gotten their soul saved, which is the renewing of their minds. They think they received the whole package when they were born again. They might have some spiritual insight into some areas, such as the gifts, and may function proficiently in that area. But sin abides in their minds, flesh and conversation. Paul made mention of this in 1 Corinthians 3:1, where he called such people "carnal" Christians, even though you will notice in Chapter 1:7, of this same book that they were behind in no gift. You will notice this again in James 1:21, where these born-again, spirit-filled believers are told that they needed to get their soul saved. (The word "soul" here also means "mind".) Jesus said in John 3:3, that that which is born of the spirit is spirit and that which is born of the flesh is flesh. The spirit and the flesh do not get saved at the same time. Jesus was saying that being born again is not a fleshly experience. The flesh will have to be worked on in a progressive manner, as the mind is reprogrammed or saved. And then we need to keep it saved by memorizing the Word of God. (See 1 Corinthians 15:2.)

Remember, Lot yielded to the first step and it cost him his most prized possessions on this earth.

Obsession –

"And it came to pass, as we went to prayer, a certain damsel possessed with a spirit of divination met us, which brought her masters much gain by soothsaying:" (Acts 16:16).

The Bible says there was a lady possessed with a spirit of divination. You will notice this lady had control over most of the faculties of her person. She never rolled on the ground, etc. This woman was possessed of the devil, but only at various times. She was in the second stage. You will also notice that some people in the second stage will have the spirit in their minds and others in their flesh.

Luke 13:16, describes her as a daughter of Abraham. So she was a child of God whom satan had bound for 18 years. You can see this lady was in love with God, but she was tormented by satan. A spirit obsessed her body. She was on her way to heaven but didn't know enough truth to set her free.

The Last Stage –

In this stage, you will notice a person has no control over his spirit, mind or body.

Mark 5, gives us an example of a person in this final stage. The unclean spirit that possessed this man caused him torment "always," day and night. This man would do things that caused great torment in his spirit, mind and body. Mark 9:17-22, tells another story of a young boy who would tear himself, gnash with his teeth, foam at the mouth, throw himself on the ground and often cast himself into fire and water in an effort to destroy himself. Again, you can see this young boy was fully possessed. It is plain that he suffered a fuller possession than the young lady of Acts 16:16.

Before we go on to the next train of thought, I want to spend a little time here to help some people. I have noticed over the years how some parents would allow their small children to get angry and throw themselves down, backwards or otherwise. This isn't anything but the very beginnings of the second stage. It isn't normal for any human being to want to hurt themselves. I have also noticed those children, when grown, are allowed to let their senses govern them rather than their parents. The same parents make those children go to school whether the children want to nor not. And the high percentage of the time it is a public school in which they are being trained 40 hours a week to act like, think like and talk like the devil. It almost seems a planned preparation for hell.

Then Sunday comes along, and the parents say, "Well,

I don't believe you should force God on anybody. I want them to make that decision on their own." It doesn't make sense – forcing children to learn to be like the devil but not training them to go to church! When I was "in training" in the military, I was made to reach a certain point of maturity, before I was put in a position to be in war and on the front line with the enemy that was out to destroy me. And if we failed our "training," we had to do it over.

By the same token, when our children are small there had better be some training going on concerning God's goodness and how to know it. God has given parents that responsibility, because children do not possess the wisdom that God has given parents. We have the repsonsibllity to get into the Word of God, find out what it has to say and train our children to abide by its principles, regardless of how unpopular it is to the world, other Christians and relatives. In the process, we parents will get into the Word, find out what is right and wrong and grow up too!

While I am here let me say something to pastors: "We spend much money and put much emphasis on foreign missions, while our children are right under our feet in our homes being trained to go to hell. I believe Jesus said - first Jerusalem then Judea? If we are not taking care of home first, we are not in the will of God. It is the church's responsibility to have Christian schools. I have never had the money to do anything God has told me to do. But if I fall down on my face before Him, somehow it gets done. One of my biggest helps in this area is making sure everything you think is yours is given to God, as His checkbook can make all the bills.

Now I want to go into another train of thought. There exists another erroneous teaching in the world today. And that is the idea that when a spirit leaves a person or is cast out, there has to be some type of manifestation such as vomiting, etc. These people base this theory on the account in Mark 9:17-22. If you notice in the Scripture this phenomena occurs only once, and then the boy didn't vomit after or during the casting out process. Scripture does not say Jesus found the boy vomiting but rather foaming at the mouth.

I believe that something of this nature could take place (someone expelling something from the mouth after a deliverance) but rest assured that when ministries are built on things of this nature, a religious spirit of deception is strongly involved. I have cast out evil spirits nearly on a daily basis since 1973 and cannot think of two situations that are alike. And I have never seen an expulsion of any kind. I have also noticed in seeing demons that I cannot ever remember any two demons looking exactly alike. In fact, most of them are extremely different in appearance and character. Something else I have noticed about these people who vomit up demons (or whatever kind of contortion they go through) – they do not get rid of the problem.

Staying Clean –

We can have a life style in which satan cannot use us. We can live as Jesus lived. We do not have to submit to the blinding pleasures of sin which, at best, are only good for a very short time and then come the wages of torment. Here are some Scriptures which will help you. I will not say too much about them as I believe I have covered this same issue earlier in this book. So go back and see what I had to say about the following Scriptures: Matthew 12:43-44; John 15:3; Romans 12:1-2; James 1:21, Isaiah 26:3; Philippians 4:8; Matthew 6:22; 1 Peter 5:7,8,9; Proverbs 16:3; Proverbs 3:24.

CHAPTER *9*

The Simplicity of Casting Out Evil Spirits

T he longer I live and the more I know about God's Word, the more I am convinced that the worst enemy is satan and that I am victorious over him by the words of my mouth. Or I can be defeated by the devil with the words of my mouth. The more knowledge of God's Word that I have and use over the enemy, the more victory I will experience.

Something else you need to know and stay on guard about is that the more knowledge you have of satan and the more you use it, the more satan will concentrate his efforts against you in an unprecedented way. Remember Revelation 12:12. In the last days the devil will see that he has but a short time and he will come down unto you having GREAT WRATH (Verse 17). This wrath is focused on those who keep the commandments of God, regardless of what any force would do to get you to think or talk to the contrary, and on those who speak them boldly in the face of defeat, knowing the true source of their problem and their victory!

Ever since I began to write this book, satan has attacked me, my family, finances and ministry in greater measure than ever before. And I have known the wrath of satan. Let me say this, there is everything to fear, yes, far beyond your imaginations, IF YOU GET IN THE BATTLE AND RETREAT. TO WHOM MUCH IS GIVEN, MUCH IS REQUIRED. But it is in the fire, storm, floods and disasters beyond your comprehension and abilities that you see Jesus!

"When thou passest through the waters, I will be with thee; and through the rivers, they shall not overflow thee: when thou walkest through the fire, thou shalt not be burned; neither shall the flame kindle upon thee.

"For I am the Lord thy God, the Holy One of Israel, thy Saviour:..." (Isaiah 43:2,3).

"So shall they fear the name of the Lord from the west, and his glory from the rising of the sun. When the enemy shall come in like a flood, the Spirit of the Lord shall lift up a standard against him," (Isaiah 59:19).

When the enemy comes in like a flood, God comes on the scene, beyond your fondest dreams. The real heroes in the battles get a special recognition from the commander-in-chief. He wants to talk to the elite of the elite, person to person.

"He that hath my commandments, and keepeth them, he it is that loveth me: and he that loveth me shall be loved of my Father, and I will love him, and will manifest myself to him," (John 14:21).

Jesus Himself said, "Those who love me will KEEP MY WORDS. And I will love them and manifest myself to them." The word "manifest" in the original Greek means, "I WILL EXHIBIT IN PERSON. I WILL APPEAR TO THEM. I WILL SHOW MYSELF TO THEM!" It is beyond your imagination the depths of "God's" lovingkindness toward you that is displayed while just in the presence of the KING OF KINGS.

Understanding The Enemy's Strategy –

The rewards are great but WE MUST UNDERSTAND THE WARFARE. As never before, satan is not playing games; he is destroying.

Years ago I noticed that from a natural standpoint, things were looking real bad in many different areas. A perception came to me with these words, "If you want to see and experience more of God's goodness and blessings, you need to go from one hour of prayer and reading the Bible per day to two hours. So I increased, only to find things getting worse. After a period of time, the perception said, "You need to add one more hour." This went on until I was spending about three hours a day, most of the time, only to find things getting worse. The voice came back to me and said, "You are in a very rough situation, so you must even do more. You need to continue what you are doing but you need to start fasting."

The voice continued week after week to influence me to fast even more to the point that I needed to fast at least 40 days and nights. Things were worse than ever. Keep in mind this had been going on for several months. I finally got very angry about the situation and yes, "very" angry with God. In desperation, I said, "I am not doing ANYTHING MORE. I am not going to read my Bible at all. I am not going to pray at all and fasting – forget it! I was mad at everything and everybody. I tried to keep it well hidden, because I had been in the ministry for several years and had no place to go or nothing else to do. I had burned all my bridges.

I believe if you are ever going to amount to anything in God, you need to burn every bridge, so that unless God comes to your rescue, there is no other hope. I would have accepted ANY KIND of employment that would have given at least the same income. This would have been very easy to do. I had given up in my mind. Then during the night session, I immediately awakened and rose up in the bed as I heard footsteps coming down the hallway in our home. I heard the footsteps approach the door, watched the doorknob turn, expecting one of our girls to walk through the doorway, only to be surprised as satan himself walked in.

Now up to this point, satan had appeared to me only two other times. And prior to this, I had experienced countless visits from evil spirits during all hours, but predominately during the night sessions. When these experiences first occurred, fear would come to the degree that I felt death was imminent. But the Lord would always speak to me, assuring me of my authority over the spirits and their purpose to destroy. Finally I matured to the point that no longer did every pore open instantly to secrete sweat faster than I ever imagined possible. Truthfully, it was amazing what their presence would cause my mind and body to do, because of their extreme, fearful torment. At times, every pore in my body would open; the hair on my body would literally stand straight up. But eventually, I matured to the place that I experienced absolutely no fear. It would be the same amount of fear you would have over a maggot. After all, satan is lord over the flies and flies are just grown-up maggots.

By this time in my life, I would not even speak audibly to them, such as calling out to them and saying, "You spirit of religion, deception, fear," or whatever type spirit it might be. All I said was, "I rebuke you in Jesus' Name." At this point, I would rarely move my body, as I had such confidence in my spirit that all the forces of hell were extremely horrified of me. This time, I rebuked satan from out of my spirit, as in times past. I simply released that authority out; but he only trembled when the Name of Jesus was thrust at him. He fought the trembling, regained his composure and his hideous grin, and then said, "You do not have authority over me because you are in disobedience. God told you to read your Bible and pray three hours a day and to fast 40 days and nights and you haven't."

In my mind I said, "He's right," and surrendered to the torment of his presence. At this point, I noticed I was totally, physically paralyzed. I tried to generate all my energies to try and move the smallest finger on my right hand and couldn't even move it a little. In my mind I thought, "How could he have known what God was telling me?"

As those moments raced through my mind, that same voice that had been speaking to me said, "In the realm of the spirit, spirits know spiritual truths. So satan knew when God spoke to you."

By experience in the realm of the spirit, I knew that volumes of information is given by being in the presence of any kind of spirit without any audible words being spoken. Mouths do not have to open for information to be given. After a very short time, satan vanished laughing at me. You talk about depressed! For several days I was extremely depressed. And you would be too if a maggot had authority over you. That was the state I was in.

Finally, I awakened out of sleep after several days of depression had passed. I was beginning to have sleepless nights. I got out of bed during the night session to go into the bathroom only to lay on the floor and weep and groan with great despondency. I cried out and said, "Lord, you know I love you more than anything or anybody. I have proven it over and over again in my lifetime."

Up to that point my wife and I had given one-fourth the value of a new home away and about one-eighth the value of another new home. My wife and I built our last home with our own hands in 1982 (about 1,800 square feet of living space). We borrowed the full amount needed to build it and gave the money away, an amount almost equal to the full price of the home since it was 85 percent paid off. We also owned five and one-half acres with it. We had given several cars away as well as a business. We had given all this because we loved and continue to love the Lord. Our lives were living sacrifices to the Lord and still are.

I cried out, "Lord, You know I will do ANYTHING for You, but You must tell me what to do." This was my heart's cry. Then I sensed the presence of Jesus Himself. This time I did not see, hear or feel His presence; but what He had to say was superior to audible words or anything else the natural senses could relate to. Even a translation to heaven would not have had more reality to the experience. Jesus said, "You are my child based upon what I have done not what you can do or have done. You have authority and all of my blessings are based upon my love for you. You do not have to do ANYTHING TO EARN WHAT I HAVE GIVEN TO YOU!"

Volumes of information raced through my being. The heavy cloud of depression left instantly and I knew once again of the unconditional, unmerited love and grace God has for all humanity. The Bible is plain when it says THE LETTER KILLETH and the Spirit giveth life. Yes, we should read our Bibles because we love God, but not to try to get God to do something He already HAS DONE. (See 1 Peter 1:2-4.)

The Priceless Inheritance –

The Bible ought to be as valued as the will of a loved one who died and left, directed toward you personally, volumes of information that bequeathed untold riches with each sentence. Information that would give you fortunes in every direction you would turn to go throughout the world.

Such is the Bible in its simplest form and so much more! Yes, we should pray, because prayer is simply an invitation for the most powerful, loving, gentle, magistrate and ruler of all existence to shower new enrichments upon your life with His divine purpose of mercy and goodness, blessings beyond your understanding and capabilities to receive. And that is His greatest desire.

"Beloved, I wish above all things that thou mayest prosper and be in health, even as thy soul prospereth," (3 John 2).

Yes, he desires to caress you afresh with His tender mercies and compassion in newer and newer depths every morning.

"It is of the Lord's mercies that we are not consumed, because his compassions fail not.

"They are new every morning: great is thy faithfulness," (Lamentations 3:22-23).

His lovingkindness is better than life. (See Psalm 63:3.) He has experiences of goodness for all of humanity that are better than anything this life could offer. Yes, better than life itself. (See Ephesians 3:19.) The Bible says that God has a love for us that passeth "all" knowledge. I asked the Lord one time, "How can this be? You have all knowledge." He replied, "If anyone ever discovers all the knowledge of love that I have for them, I'll make some more!"

Yes, we should fast but not to get God's attention. Rather, we should fast because we are so in love with Him that we just forget to eat.

I was free at this point, more so than I ever had been in my life. I simply lived in the presence of this grace, goodness and freedom for a couple of weeks. Then again I was awakened during the night session. When you experience the realm of the spirit, both of God and satan, you will find when you are awakened, you are more alert than at any natural time in your life. More alert than you are in the prime of your day. So I was awakened, hearing the same footsteps I had heard just a couple of weeks earlier.

Everything was the same. Satan opened the door and walked in with the same demonic, smirky grin. I rebuked him only out of my spirit just as before. This time he trembled greatly and forced the grin to stay on his face and said, "You have no authority over me. You didn't the last time I was here, and you're worse off now than before. You haven't read your Bible on a daily basis ONCE since I last saw you. You are not spending any time in prayer and haven't fasted a bite as God told you to."

Satan was right. I hadn't done any of that. In fact, I had gained a little weight. But I knew what Jesus said, and knew it was sound doctrine. The most sound doctrine in existence is that we are saved, a child of God and a partaker of His divine nature by unmerited favor or grace. So I released out of my spirit these words: "Satan, I have authority over you in every situation. I have this authority, not because of my prayer life, not because of how much I read the Bible or how much I fast. I have authority over you because of what Jesus has done, not what I could ever do. I was born into this life style. Now leave in Jesus' Name!"

If you notice, I only said what Jesus said – just repeated what Jesus had told me. It's easy to enforce someone else's power which has been proven for multitudes of years. At that point, in the realm of the spirit, I felt all of hell just tremble and shake, and I have not seen any entity experience so much fear. And he hasn't been back since. He's afraid. He still sends his imps to do his dirty work; but he hasn't showed up. Just talking about it makes me want to dance.

For years I have wanted people to see into the spirit realm as I do for the purpose of understanding it, understanding true warfare, evil forces and how they are defeated when a child of God knows and uses the Word of God against them. So I pray this book will help in this respect. The world needs to know the truth and the truth will set them free.

Satan Has Been Put to Nought –

"And having spoiled principalities and powers, he made a shew of them openly, triumphing over them in it," (Colossians 2:15).

Satan and his imps have been spoiled, put to nought or paralyzed, all co-equal terms in the Greek. Jesus paralyzed satan and his kingdom when He arose from the dead. If satan is paralyzed, why is he so powerful? Very simple – he uses the power God has given the church and perverts it. And Christians are responsible. Let me give you an illustration.

Let's assume you walk into a room and see a being sitting in the middle of the room. He "appears" to be 20 feet tall. You notice that his physique gives the impression that he could lift the largest building in the world or perhaps outrun a jet plane. He speaks in a loud gruesome voice saying, "I am going to twist both your legs off and then beat you with them."

Immediately fear grips your heart and you tremble and make plans for torment and death. But then, in walks a little lady who weighs about 90 pounds, carrying a ten-pound Bible, so marked up in its pages. She says to the large, beastly-appearing, evil entity: "Shut your mouth. You're not doing ANYTHING." And the being trembles and shakes while apologizing. Then the little lady turns to you and says, "I want you to know some truths that will show you that you never have to fear this being again; because he will relive this moment over and over again. Number One, he is paralyzed. The only thing he can move is his mouth. Number 2, he is sitting behind a type of glass that enlarges his appearance at least 20 times."

Do you get the picture? Satan is a liar and the glass he

sits behind is the mental pictures he has given you. The Bible says in Romans 1:16 and Matthew 22:29, that the Scriptures, God's Word, are the power of God. And the Bible says death and life are in the power of the tongue. So if you let satan get hold of power which was meant to bless you, he will pervert it to destroy you. You will also notice that Mark 11:24, says we can have whatsoever we say, negative or positive.

In a great sense, many destroy themselves. Psalms 17:3, says that with the words of my lips I am delivered from the destroyer. (Also see Proverbs 6:2; John 10:10; and Proverbs 18:21.) The same pistol that is purposed to protect me, when in the hands of the enemy, will destroy me.

There are people today who really fight the doctrine of having what you say. God has intended for this doctrine to bless humanity. But you will notice the ones who fight it are into doctrines of man, and they believe in it more than the ones who use it for good. The negative group that fights it is always going around saying negative things like, "I'll always be sick, poor, etc." And they always have JUST WHAT THEY SAY. They really believe in what they say; they really do believe their words. So satan has been given permission, by them, to promote his negative, evil kingdom. If Christians would just believe in the simplicity of the Word! Psalms 119:130, says the entrance of His Words gives light and understanding to the simple. If it isn't simple, God isn't in it!

Deliverance By Our Words –

"For a certain woman, whose young daughter had an unclean spirit, heard of him, and came and fell at his feet:

"The woman was a Greek, a Syrophenician nation; and she besought him that he would cast forth the devil

111

out of her daughter.

"But Jesus said unto her, Let the children first be filled: for it is not meet to take the children's bread, and to cast it unto the dogs.

"And she answered and said unto him, Yes, Lord: yet the dogs under the table eat of the children's crumbs.

"And he said unto her, For this saying go thy way; the devil is gone out of thy daughter," (Mark 7:25-29).

Notice here that this woman's daughter was 30 to 120 miles away. Another notable factor is that the Syrophenician woman wasn't a Christian. You will also notice that she didn't pray. Jesus didn't pray nor did He exercise any authority. This woman's daughter wasn't delivered because of her holiness or right standing with God. Keep in mind this woman was a sinner. But notice Jesus said, BECAUSE OF THE WORDS OF THIS WOMAN'S MOUTH, her daughter, though 30 to 120 miles away, was delivered from demonic, tormenting powers. Words that are in agreement with God's Words, no matter who uses them, cannot return void.

"So shall my word be that goeth forth out of my mouth: it shall not return unto me void, but it shall accomplish that which I please; and it shall prosper in the thing whereto I sent it," (Isaiah 55:11).

Can you see why satan fights the doctrine of confession so hard? In Daniel 10, you see this same doctrine established. An angel (a spirit) from heaven, the abode of God, came to accomplish Daniel's words. Keep in mind, one-third of heaven's angels fell with satan, but they still function in the same manner they were created. THEY COME FOR WORDS – TO ACCOMPLISH THEM.

The same degree to which we get serious with believing and speaking God's Word is the same degree to which we will experience victory over defeat from satan.

Love Stops Satan –

In Ephesians 3:18,19, the Bible talks about a breadth, depth, length and height to knowing the love of God that passeth knowledge.

We understand that God is the most intelligent being in existence. Understanding that, why would He talk about five dimensions, when the most intelligent human being can only understand, relate to and believe in a three-dimensional world? In the study of geometry, there are only three dimensions. In essence, the laws of geometry can only agree upon a tangible substance. In the study of geometry there are dimensional laws. The first dimensionnal world is controlled by the second and the third; and the second is controlled by the third.

In the Scriptures, God gives two more dimensions beyond that which the natural man can relate to or accept. I find the word "depth" in the Greek has the meaning of being proud, mysterious, the deep things. And as I understand this dimension, I find it is the realm of the spiritual. The natural mind cannot relate to the realm of the spiritual. God's Word, angelic beings and evil, demonic beings are of this dimension. Notice Ephesians 6:19. Here the Gospel is the mystery. Also keep in mind the laws of geometry in which the laws of the first is ruled by the second and so forth.

So the spiritual world controls the three-dimensional or natural world. Let us go further to the fifth dimension about which God's Word speaks. Ephesians 3:19, reveals that the love of God is the fifth dimension. And in perfect agreement with the Word of God, God's love fulfills the whole counsel of God. (See Romans 13:10, Matthew 22:36-40.) So, in turn, love controls and rules over the other dimensional worlds. Now we can see why God put in His Word the other two dimensions. But I believe there is still yet a higher reason; and that reason is this: love rules over satan and his dimension or kingdom.

If the most intelligent person in the world would be confronted with the fourth dimensional world, he would be tormented by it because he would be unable to understand or relate to it in any way. He could not even believe it exists. For example, if a spirit would appear to him, its appearance would torment him to instant defeat. In like manner, satan does not have knowledge of nor can he relate to the realm of the fifth dimension. He doesn't even believe it exists. Only God and his children can abide in this dimension. When satan is confronted with the fifth dimension it is sort of like the most intelligent person being confronted with the spirit world, or the fourth dimensional world, when he doesn't even understand, relate to or even believe in spirits. Only when satan is confronted with love (AGAPE) is it supernaturally compounded in torment. Not that God's intention is to torment anyone. His purpose is to bless.

But stop and think – if someone came into your presence during the night session after your eyes had been accustomed to darkness for a few hours, bringing an extremely bright light to give you direction, if you didn't want the direction, the light intended for blessing would be torment. Satan has been living in supernatural darkness for at least thousands of years, and God's love is the brightest light in existence. Furthermore, the devil doesn't want any direction from God. So God's love brings him supernatural torment. Following are some Scriptures that demonstrate this truth: Mark 3:10, 11; 5:1-15; Matthew 8:29; Luke 4:40; and Mark 3:10.

You will notice that Jesus did not rebuke these spirits with words from His mouth. There was no sign of any physical action whatsoever. The only thing that happened was that living love confronted the demonic kingdom, and the demons were tormented and cast out. They left the presence of Jesus. Darkness fled in the presence of light. The fifth dimension just supernaturally ruled over the fourth dimension.

"Submit yourselves therefore to God. Resist the devil, and he will flee from you," (James 4:7).

Submit to God (AGAPE LOVE) resist the devil, and he will flee as in terror. The Scriptures I gave you previously about Jesus confronting those who were demon possessed, should be read in different versions such as the Amplified Bible. In so doing, you will notice in greater detail that these spirits would scream, shriek and would literally say, "Torment me not!" Love's torment overrules satan and his kingdom!

CHAPTER 10

The Armor of God

Romans 8:37, says we are more than conquerors through Him who loves us. As you read on in this chapter, you will notice that neither death, life, angels principalities, powers, things present nor things to come can separate us from the love of God. If we can learn how much God loves us, death, with its greatest threat, is nothing; we have power over it. Life's greatest source of energy and power is rendered helpless when trying to defeat us, when we know how much God loves us. The greatest forces of hell are as an ant trying to overcome a lion when they try to overcome a child of God who is hidden and sheltered in the secret place where God's love is saturating them. There has never been anything nor will there ever be anything that could be victorious over the child of God who knows he is the apple of his Father's eye.

Understanding how much God loves you is a great step, maybe the greatest step, in having victory in every area of thinking. It is having the most powerful being in existence as your Father; and He is enforcing the fact that anything or anybody who would try to come against you must go through Him first.

Victory Through God's Armor –

Ephesians 6:10, urges that we be strong in the Lord. In essence, allow your being to be yielded fully in His power. The Bible teaches us something like 400 times in the Scriptures that we are to be in the Lord, in Christ. If we are in Christ, "WE ARE IN HIS ARMOR." Ephesians 6:11, teaches us to put on the Lord's armor. If we will get in Christ, we will be in His armor. The more knowledge we have to be in Christ, the more of God's armor we will wear. To know what God's Word says and do it, letting it BE IN YOUR LIFE, causes you to be in God's armor. See, you're doing the Word on the outside because it is within you. This is wearing God's armor.

Philippians 4:13, says we can do all things THROUGH CHRIST who strengthens us. Looking at God's armor (Ephesians 6:13,14) teaches us that, after we have put on God's armor and have been active with it, then we just stand. Having done all to stand with God in armor (doing the Word) then just stand. Something else you will notice is that God does not have any armor for the back. And as you study the Word of God, you can understand why. You do everything that it says you can do, and then you just stand in the middle of the battlefield with such dignity, confidence and understanding of who you are, that nothing could possibly come against you!

Once we put God's armor on, the only time we will experience defeat is when we turn our backs on God. God doesn't even prepare for defeat or retreat. Paul said in 1 Timothy 1:18,19, that those who HAVE WARRED A GOOD WARFARE (and there is only one "good" kind of warfare and that's one you win) and then turn away, WILL MAKE SHIPWRECK! When you have used the power of God against satan and have done harm to his kingdom and then turn your back on that power, which is God's Word, then you are heading for disaster of your own making.

"For I am not ashamed of the gospel of Christ: for it is the power of God unto salvation to every one that believeth;..." (Romans 1:16).

So many times we think we do not need to continue soaking up God's goodness from His Word. We think we can get by on yesterday's or last year's knowledge of God's goodness in His Word. But my Bible teaches me that my trust, my belief, my faith in God comes from CONTINU-ALLY GIVING AUDIENCE to God's Word. "Not" just from having heard. Yes, continually reading, hearing, thinking on God's Word.

Understanding the Armor –

Ephesians 6:14, teaches us to have our loins girt about with truth. As you understand the human body, the loin area is located from the lower ribs to the hip area. This is the power portion of the body of a soldier which allows him to advance to the degree of strength he possesses. The more powerful a person is in this area, the more ground he can cover. The Bible says to girt or protect this area with truth.

There is no greater truth than God's Word. So you can take kingdoms, lands, etc., according to the degree that the Word promises you those areas. In other words, the far-away victories that other people do not even know exist, can be won by you to the degree of knowledge you possess in God's Word! Jesus said in Matthew 12:12, that the kingdom of heaven suffereth violence and the violent take it by force. There are times when we are supposed to just stand our ground. And we need to find Scripture to support those stands we must take.

But we need to equally know that there are Scriptures to support us TAKING some things that belong to us. Sometimes we need to be aggressive! In fact I would have very little in life if I didn't just get out there and act like God's Word was true. Yes, get out there where the devil and circumstances are screaming that you are crazy, as well as quite a few Christians. Sort of like Peter – yes, he sank BUT HE DID WALK ON THE WATER. The same opportunity was offered to the other ten spectators in the boat. If you are incredibly strong and protected in all areas of your life, but are weak in your loins, you'll not achieve much unless you girt yourself with some truth that promises ownership of distant kingdoms.

The Breastplate of Righteousness –

The breastplate is the armor that protects one of the most vital areas of your person. In fact, instant wounding in the breast area is instant wounding of the heart. And we know that an instant wound to the head or the heart is instant defeat. If this area is not covered, you will die prematurely. The better this area is covered, the better your longevity in battle. And as long as you are on this earth, you will be in battle.

We must know that we are in right standing with our heavenly Father. This will cause a great deal of divine confidence to come when in battles of life. It helps to know our purpose and strength in battle which is the righteousness of God in Christ.

"For he hath made him to be sin for us, who knew no sin; that we might be made the righteousness of God in him," (2 Corinthians 5:21).

The word "righteous" also means holy, pure, having the reputation of God. There is only one way you can get that and that is by God's grace! By His grace, He said it. Ephesians 1:18, also supports this train of thought which was detailed earlier in this book. Knowing you have the Reputation of God will create great Holy Ghost, divine boldness to stand in any battle this life or principalities

119

could offer you.

Many people are afraid of the devil, but when you begin to understand the armor of God, you look for the devil to stop his evil deed.

Feet Shod –

Verse 15 of Ephesians 6, says we are to have our feet shod with the preparation of the Gospel. Every place we go, we are prepared to give only GOOD NEWS! An elite soldier will have to walk through mud, through areas which may appear to cause him to stink, through fire and through storms, because the battle rages on and victory is on the other side of the fire. Yes, the elite of the elite NEVER once have anything to say but GOOD NEWS, A GOOD REPORT!

Smith Wigglesworth once said it like this: we need to be so full of God's love, that we are like a dry sponge soaked in oil. When it is thrown against the wall, stepped on, squeezed roughly or abused in any fashion, the only thing that comes out is the oil of God's love. Love never fails. (See 1 Corinthians 13:8.) When torment comes, people will say, "Did you see how far that oil squirted when that sponge was jumped on?" Attention is on the oil. It will soak people far away to the degree of oil within.

Shield of Faith –

Verse 17 of Ephesians 6, says to "take" the helmet of salvation. A helmet will protect the part of the body that is as vital as the heart. So we need to keep our brain saved (safe). We need to keep our brains protected. 1 Corinthians 15:2, says we are saved (healed, healthy, of sound mind, financially blessed, delivered and protected) IF WE KEEP GOD'S WORD IN MEMORY. When you forget what God's Word says, you will be defeated in that area of your life. *So salvation is lost when memory is lost.* James

1:21, teaches us that after a person is born again and spirit filled, he is to have his soul (brain) saved. Romans 12:1,3, teaches us the same truth – of being not conformed to this world but being conformed to the realm of God, so we can know the good, acceptable and perfect will of God. There is only one way you can know God's will – you have to read it first. (Also see Ephesians 1:9; 3:4; 5:17.)

Another truth I want to bring out is that the word "transformed" is exactly the same root word in the Greek as "transfigured" in Matthew 9:2, where Jesus was transfigured before his disciples and his clothing and person was shining exceedingly white as snow. So we can see the splendor and importance of renewing (saving the mind) with God's Word. We would be like Jesus, in a transfigured state, that the Father be glorified. So when satan sees you coming, he thinks God is coming because you are wearing God's armor.

The Sword –

Of all the armor you will notice, this is the only weapon God gives us. It is His Word. Jesus said to satan in Matthew 4:4, "It is written," and this defeated satan. Something you might have already noticed is everything about God's armor has to do with His Word. It is knowing what part of God's Word to use when, how and what kind of results you can expect from it. But it is so important to know God's Word well enough that, when in battle, you do not have the helmet on your feet, etc. If people would understand that in a lifetime one cannot fully understand all of God's goodness from His Word, they would start making their children go to Bible school 40 hours a week for 13 years and then on into advanced Bible college after that. His Words are LIFE in its greatest sense to those who find them.

"The way of the wicked is as darkness: they know not

at what they stumble.

"My son, attend to my words; incline thine ear unto my saying.

"Let them not depart from thine eyes; keep them in the midst of thine heart.

"For they are life unto those that find them, and health to all their flesh.

"Keep thy heart with all diligence; for out of it are the issues of life," (Poverbs 4:19-23).

The things revealed, written down, belong to us and our children.

> *"The secret things belong unto the Lord our God: but those things which are revealed belong unto us and to our children for ever, that we may do all the words of this law,"* (Deuteronomy 29:29).

I call heaven and earth together against you that I have set before you life and death, blessing or cursing. Therefore, you choose. (See Deuteronomy 30:19.)

Praying –

I have covered much of this train of thought throughout this book. So let me just make this little expansion.

Pray always, which is communication with a loving, heavenly Father who wants to enhance your life beyond your imagination. When you have a close communication with the Lord, there isn't any type of an evil spirit that could ever get close to even setting up an ambush against you. Why? Because, the Lord will tell you about it first. And don't forget the tranquil life style that will be yours.